The Art of Rocket Science
Book 2
Winning Competitive Pursuits for Technical Services

CHARLES MCINTYRE
and
HAROLD GLASER

Copyright © 2014 Charles McIntyre and Harold Glaser
All rights reserved.
ISBN-13: 978-1499574791

CONTENTS

Acknowledgments — i

1. Introduction: The Art of Selling Rocket Science — 1
2. Building Effective Relationships — 5
3. Competitive Strategies for Winning Pursuits — 29
4. Positioning to Improve Your Chance of Winning — 47
5. Understanding Selection Processes — 68
6. The Dynamics of Selection Committees — 83
7. The Mechanics of Proposal Production — 93
8. Winning Presentations and Interviews — 111
9. Closing the Deal — 130
10. Annotated Bibliography — 142

About the Authors — 146

ACKNOWLEDGMENTS

We are grateful for our families,
colleagues, and clients, and we acknowledge that we
learned everything we know from them.

Chapter 1
Introduction: The Art of Selling Rocket Science

> *"Instead of playing to win, I was playing not to lose. It reminds me of the story I once heard about two friends being chased by a bear, when one turned to the other and said, "I just realized that I don't need to outrun the bear; I only need to outrun you."*
> — Sean Covey, The 7 Habits Of Highly Effective Teens[1]

After a meeting at our company's headquarters, we found ourselves alone with the president of the firm. In public and in large meetings, he was a jovial father figure to employees and a confident leader to customers and peers. But on the few occasions when we were alone with him, he let his guard down. "I'm worried," he said. "Our people have great skills and provide terrific service, but they have become 'order-takers.' They wait for clients to give them projects; they don't seek out interesting opportunities and knock down the competition to get those jobs."

We knew what he was talking about. How do you light the competitive spirit in technical professionals to win the best and biggest projects? "Sit down," we said. "Let's talk about this."

As we described in our first book: *Building a Sales Program for Technical Services*, the practice of selling consumer goods and products has been a mature profession for many years. The battles between manufacturers of snack foods are textbook examples of effective marketing strategy. But equally interesting to us are the sale and marketing of technical services, such as engineering, architecture, applied science, information technology, management consulting, and niches within law and finance. Publications focused on these professions have been largely ab-

---

[1] Covey, Sean. *The 7 Habits of Highly Effective Teens: The Miniature Edition: The Ultimate Teenage Success Guide*. Philadelphia: Running, 2002.

sent from our libraries and classrooms. Our intent is to reverse that trend with our first book, dedicated to building a sales operation at a technical services firm, combined with the book you are reading on the topic of winning competitive pursuits.

Both of these books support our main themes that the marketing and sales of complex, technical services (rocket science) are distinctly different from simpler consumer services. The professionals who provide these services earn their livings by developing solutions to complex problems, <u>and</u> are also asked to participate in selling their services to customers. Because of the human factors in making buying choices, we contend there is *art* combined with the selling and buying of *science*.

<u>We titled the series *The Art of Selling Rocket Science* because we're fascinated with the marriage of *science* and *creativity* to connect highly technical professional services and the human side of how people make choices.</u>

The first book speaks directly to technical professionals and to the marketing teams who support them. It established the importance of understanding the sales process and learning to be proficient at business development. In addition, we outlined:

- An argument against the conventional wisdom of technologists that being smarter is better.
- The methodology, structure and planning required for a successful sales and marketing program.
- How to plan proactively in selecting clients that fit your goals, the culture of your firm, and the type of people you employ.
- Client service: how it parallels the performance of technical work, and the role that good or bad client service can play in your ability to win new work.
- The money side, the need for systems, and how developing and promoting your brand will provide a foundation for marketing and sales.
- Perspective on conferences and trade shows, which attract inordinate attention from engineers and scientists, and developing techniques for gaining the most value from your investment.

This next book, *Winning Competitive Pursuits for Technical Services*, dives deeper into the Art and Science of seeking out new opportunities and beating the competition to win those projects. We create methodologies for:

- Building relationships with clients and the emotional side of complex projects.
- Creating competitive strategies that rally people toward a common goal of understanding the client's needs and differentiating yourself from the rest of the pack.
- Combining your relationships and your strategy to "position" your firm in the weeks and months prior to the formal competition and improve your chance of winning.
- Understanding selection processes and the dynamics of selection committees to better appreciate the human element in making choices.
- We present the practical details of proposal and interview production, along with structure for getting the most out of your key team members.
- Lastly, we discuss how to close the deal, and deliver a signed contract in the face of events which can occur late in the decision-making process.

In both of these companion books, we make the strong case for bringing together the technical and non-technical professionals to make an unbeatable team. Whether you are a buyer or seller, marketer or scientist, engineer or writer, we know that the combination of strong left and right brain thinking is powerful, and proven to be an effective cornerstone in long-term business success for your company and your clients.

We assert that the strongest careers are built by people who combine strong technical skills with creative sales strategies that deliver the best value for meeting customers' unmet needs. Teaching technical staff to step outside of their hard-wired DNA of solution-based thinking, to recognize the human side of making choices will result in customers lining up for your services.

Moreover, this combination of technical and non-technical skills will also benefit you by placing you in the driver's seat of a career path toward the choicest clients and most prestigious projects. In short, we contend that if the principles presented in both books are applied, the reader will achieve success through the appropriate balance of art and science, in the best interest of the buyer.

> We talked to the CEO for several hours. We spoke about the personality of the technical people in the company. "Correct," we said. "They don't seem to be effective salespeople. But we can take advantage of their natural ability to be hard working, logical, and diligent. These are all skills that are valuable in beating the competition. All we need to add is a methodology for them to follow, in co-ordination with the support of creative Marketers."
>
> He looked at us and smiled. "All right, guys. Let's get started."

Chapter 2
Building Effective Relationships

"The most important single ingredient in the formula of success is knowing how to get along with people."
– Theodore Roosevelt

> One of the company's oldest and most cherished clients had issued an RFP for a major study to upgrade a facility. This was not only a project worth several million dollars, but strategic as well. The successful firm would be ideally positioned for future work. In addition, the technical issues to be addressed would likely lead to similar engagements with other clients.
>
> As could be expected, this pursuit was highly competitive. And, to boot, this was a public agency with oversight by a city council in a highly political environment. Past history strongly suggested that at least one or more competitors would contact council members to influence the selection process. We knew that this approach could be highly risky to relationships with staff. But we wanted to win badly. We knew a number of the council members ourselves, and had met the mayor several times. What to do?

We can talk until we turn blue about strategy, process, techniques, and tools, but the most meaningful variable that differentiates winning or losing a project opportunity is the relationship you have with your intended client. You only succeed when your client says they are eager (not just willing) to work with you. The ability to develop and maintain effective relationships is the one skill that is essential to the selling of technical services. And unfortunately, relationship-building is the skill that is most difficult to teach—difficult because those who are challenged by it are generally missing a key ingredient that is closely linked to learning—self-awareness.

Of course, relationship-building falls squarely on the *art* side of selling *rocket science*. In building relationships, we're not talking about becoming a schmoozing social butterfly or acquiring the magnetic personality of a movie star; we're talking about effectively communicating-- developing an awareness of how you're perceived by the people with whom you interact, then adjusting your communication style based on your audience's reactions. This involves pushing aside the mirror of self-indulgence to become empathetic to other people's thoughts and feelings. Simple, isn't it? It's a matter of awareness, empathy, and a healthy dose of listening to voices other than your own.

And based on our experience with technical people, self-indulgence is rooted in technology. We've spoken before about the reverence paid to technical education obtained in school, and infatuation with reaching the perfect answer. Building relationships allows technical people to see beyond the immediacy of technical problems and solutions, into a more personal world of needs, wants, hopes, and fears.

Effective communication with people results in effective relationships. The two are linked; the first is the switch that activates the second. Once established, effective communication leads to persuasion. And persuading a client to select you and your firm is your job. Whether you're the president of the firm or a marketing coordinator, your job is to convince your prospective client to select your firm, and **it is the most significant responsibility of your position**. Every skill you possess can be delegated or replaced, except your ability to connect the firm's services to the needs of the people with whom YOU have relationships.

Inside your firm and outside, your effectiveness hinges on your ability to build a wide and deep network of relationships. Wide, so that you have the best possible chance of connecting with someone who has a need for a solution you may be able to provide; deep, so that, once you've made the connection, you have the best possible chance of your solution being chosen. And you have to realize that there are a large number of competitors trying to do exactly the same thing with the same people. Salespeople who have an ability to be seen as a valued partner on their client's teams will be the most successful. Those people who gravitate toward endless conversations about themselves will bump into a ceiling above which they will never rise.

One-On-One Relationships

The sacred bond of technical services is the one between the client and the service provider's manager. Nearly all the energy of the firm is directed toward developing and supporting these relationships. The marketing success of a firm is dependent on the quality of the relationships maintained by its client managers, balanced by the skills the firm provides. Therefore, it is critical for a firm to expect its sales force to be able to develop productive relationships. In addition, it is critical that the supporting staff members, from accounting to human resources to office managers to the CEO, are all focused on protecting that bond between the client and the firm's contact points.

But where do these client managers learn their skills? Certainly, Client Management is taught at many firms, but the curriculum we are talking about is more along the lines of Relationships 101. Most professionals look toward several models: their relationships with their parents, their spouses, their friends, or their bosses as examples on which to base a relationship with a client. Invariably, without training, a professional can easily fall into one of several categories of behavior that result in unsuccessful relationships with clients. These categories described below, while stereotypical, shine a light on types of behavior that are usually unsuccessful attempts to establish relationships.

The Know-it-All, by nature, doesn't listen. This type of behavior is an attempt at building a relationship in the only way many extremely knowledgeable people know —by redistributing that knowledge to others. Know-it-Alls are so enchanted with their stellar technical abilities that they have an overpowering urge to explain the origin of the Universe (and everything in it) to their clients. This is an easy rut to fall into. The Know-it-All, often misguidedly, wants to be essential to clients by telling them how much the client doesn't know.

Because of this tendency to "explain," we believe the most valuable skill to develop to counteract this is the art of listening. Continuous talking inhibits the ability to listen and, therefore, to develop an understanding of the client's needs. By always talking, they cannot satisfy those needs.

People in the technical services profession, by nature, usually have more knowledge than the people to whom they are selling their services. However, clients are not seeking to become equally educated in these skills; they are in search of someone who can help them address their overall challenges. A technical professional can only satisfy a need if they understand what it is, in all its complexity. Developing an understanding involves listening, asking clarifying questions, thinking about what has been heard, inquiring some more, then engaging with clients to develop specific solutions.

How do you know if you have a bit of this character in your bloodstream? Ask yourself: do you know the favorite coffee drink of the receptionist in your office? You should ask. Do you know what college your marketing coordinator attended? Take a baby step—ask. Do you know what worry keeps your client awake at night? Ask the question, then close your mouth and listen. Successful business developers have the self-awareness to see this tendency within them, and compensate for it by developing listening skills (as expertly taught by Mandeville, for example. See our Annotated Bibliography for information on this worthwhile resource).

Are there exceptions? Of course. We have seen some of the most self-centered people become extraordinary business developers, by being single-mindedly, selfishly devoted to their clients. The downside is that often they don't include the rest of the firm in the relationship, therefore not taking advantage of the talent and skill available in a broader team.

What if your client is the Know-it-All? You can identify, for example, their need to see empirical data before they are persuaded. Or perhaps they need to be a part of a decision-making process to feel as if they arrived at the answer on their own, rather than fully trusting a consultant to provide a "black box" solution.

Another example is **The Buddy.** The first instinct of many people is to think that the best way to gain the confidence of a client is to be their best friend. Buddies send jokes to clients and think they're building a productive relationship. Buddies sit in a client's office and talk about their most recent Large Mouth Bass catch. Like painting a house without priming it, the Buddy System is a quick and easy way for a sociable professional to develop a relationship. Of course, making friends with a client is by no means a negative. But this is a path that often leads to an out-of-balance partnership in which the Buddy creates a friend, but not a paying client. A technical professional is offering a highly specialized service. By focusing too heavily on the social aspects of the relationship, the service provider can often be seen as too familiar, leading to the possibility of the client not taking the provider's level of expertise seriously.

More importantly, a relationship that is too focused on personal connection can put the client in a compromising position during a rigorous selection process. Ironically, the perception of a conflict of interest by the client's colleagues may result in the client intentionally lowering the scores of his Buddy's proposal to maintain his more important relationships with his co-workers and superiors.

We've seen successful business developers who have hosted city council members in their hot tubs, debating the finer points of scotch and cigars. But that familiarity was based on years of experience. In addition, the social aspects of relationship-building must always be balanced with a strict understanding that if no value is ultimately offered by the technical professional, then all he will receive for his effort will be wrinkled skin and wet towels.

The Pushover has learned, through trial and error that many clients are extremely appreciative when you do absolutely everything they request, without question. The Pushover has found that giving clients pro bono work is a way to befriend them. While providing advice and preliminary work products to a client is a legitimate way to showcase your firm's abilities, the Pushover's approach sets in motion a relationship that is out of balance from the start. The client/service provider relationship is one of carefully balanced trust, respect, and mutual need. Providing too much free advice undercuts the monetary value you place on your services.

Pushovers frequently invest their time in clients who have no intention of securing a mutually beneficial relationship; it's all one way. This time sink is the same as free service; it's a cost to the company with no return in sight. But the Pushover values the attention and appreciation, rather than the quality of the relationship and the value it provides to both parties. Relationships with clients must provide mutually beneficial results within a finite period of time. We know a large number of client managers who have "good" relationships with many clients who provide absolutely no work to the firm.

The Distant Cousin is an introvert who doesn't fully connect with the concept of being an externally focused, sales-oriented manager. This is a person for whom meeting new people takes concerted effort; not unusual, especially in the technical professions. Many people are forced into sales positions to jumpstart their careers, then are not educated or supported in developing the skills necessary to make a successful transition. While many become successful, some are left to flounder and fashion a career in which they believe they are developing a network of relationships, but in fact are seen as distant cousins to potential clients, only seen at "family" functions, such as pre-proposal meetings.

Many firms make the mistake of forcing every technical professional in the firm to become salespeople. Unfortunately, this can dilute the sales talent pool and reduce productivity. However, nearly every technical professional will play some role in client interaction, and this skill can be learned. **What many people in the profession don't understand, and is one of the reasons we wrote this book, is that building productive business relationships is a skill that can be developed, and that is inherent in almost everyone.**

Even the most introverted technical professional should be able to cultivate effective relationships for their firm. Our industry has established professional associations and conferences, for example, for the sole purpose of making it easy for technical professionals to gather with colleagues and potential clients. A firm must recognize which staff members have the propensity to be Distant Cousins and work with them on techniques to break out of that mold.

If the above examples, admittedly stereotypes, are models to be avoided, then what does a positive role model look like?

Connectors[2] listen more than they talk (unlike the Know-it-All) and understand the need for relationships that are mutually beneficial (unlike the Buddy and the Pushover), and have the skills to develop deep, committed partnerships (unlike the Distant Cousin). When listening, a business developer who is a Connector searches for ways to connect a person's need to a solution or another person that can satisfy that need.

The Connector listens, for example, to a municipal administrator from a small city that complains about the high cost of electricity and connects that complaint to a person or situation within the Connector's base of knowledge. Perhaps the Connector's firm has retrofitted another City's heating system to use electricity generated from methane gas produced at the City's wastewater treatment plant. An obvious connection, for sure, but habitually connecting challenges and opportunities is the role of the business developer—and the most distant connections are often the most valuable, because fewer people can make the same leap.

The English author E.M. Forster wrote a novel called "Howards End" with an epigraph of two words: "Only connect..."[3] The words are taken from a chapter in the book in which a woman wants to tell a man

---

[2] Gladwell, Malcolm. The Tipping Point: How Little Things Can Make a Big Difference. Boston: Little, Brown, 2000.

[3] Forster, Edward Morgan. Howards End. London: Arnold, 1910.

whom she loves what she believes is the purpose of life. She wants him to connect to the world, be a part of it, and be a part of her life. The quote has been used in other situations, such as the secret of good writing. Writing is the art of connecting the right words together, then sentences, then ideas and stories. With regard to business relationships, we use the phrase "only connect" to mean that the technical service provider is the connection between a client's needs and your company's solutions.

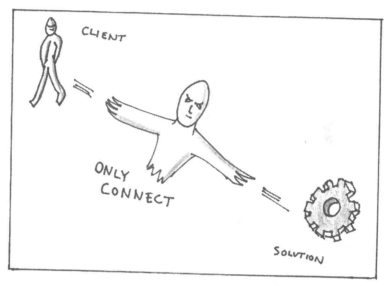

Yes, many technical professionals haven't read 19th Century English novels. That's a different point. A great business developer can make connections between seemingly disparate ideas because they have a wide range of experience, contacts, interests, and knowledge.

Yet, there is a danger in connecting a challenge and a solution too quickly. The Know-it-All is too quick to tell clients how to "fix" their problems. A person can only value advice if they trust the person delivering it. This is a key point. Trust must come first or the advice will be discounted. And it needs to be continually monitored with probing questions, because the listener moves in and out of trust as the "solution" is revealed. This takes time and can't be done over a rubber chicken dinner at a conference.

The **Trusted Advisor**[4] is thepinnacle of effective business relationships. As eloquently described by David H. Maister, Charles H. Green, and

---

[4] Maister, David H., Charles H. Green, and Robert M. Galford. The Trusted Advisor. New York: Free, 2000

Robert M. Galford in their book of the same title, the Trusted Advisor is the service provider who has nurtured a relationship in which the client has become fully open to a true partnership. An appreciation for the amount of time required to achieve a trusting, working relationship is presented in the following passage:

> *In romance, there are rules of sequence. Certain stages of the relationship are not appropriate until other stages have been met and passed. Just as there are certain expectations that are unreasonable on a first date, but not after the fifth year, there are expectations in business that vary by stage of relationship.*
>
> *The most common violation of this sequencing is the rush to give answers. It can be unsettling to find that the client is primarily interested in having his or her problem understood, in all its emotional and political complexity, as a precondition to having the problem diagnosed and solved.*

In return, the Trusted Advisor holds himself/herself responsible to not overstep the bounds of the relationship. We urge you to read this book and delve into the concept.

Another great resource is the concept of the **Servant-Leader.** Robert Greenleaf, author of Servant Leadership[5], arrived at the concept of the servant as leader partly based on reading from the works of Hermann Hesse (yes, we know, another novelist). In the fictional Journey to the East[6], Hesse plots a story in which a servant is recognized as a true leader of a group of travelers. The group only realizes this fact after the "servant" has left the group and they find themselves in chaos. Greenleaf used that metaphorical story to illustrate the complexity of relationships. According to his essay, Greenleaf described servant leadership as:

> *The servant-leader is servant first... It begins with the natural feeling that one wants to serve, to serve first. Then conscious choice brings one to aspire to lead. That person is sharply different from one who is leader first... The difference manifests itself in the care taken by the servant-- first to make sure that other people's highest priority needs are being served.*

---

[5] Greenleaf, Robert K. Servant Leadership: A Journey into the Nature of Legitimate Power and Greatness. New York: Paulist, 1977.

[6] Hesse, Hermann. The Journey to the East. New York: Noonday, 1957.

Certainly, the service provider's relationship with a person who is willing to pay for that service means that there is an inherent "compact" between them that appears obvious—one of them is the leader (the buyer) and one is the servant (the service provider). But that is a misreading of the concept. Just as the servant in the story, we are often playing roles within roles, regardless of hierarchy or seniority. In addition, we are often asked to constantly change roles, based on the task at hand, i.e. sometimes you may be a project manager, and other times a technical advisor. Both externally and internally, being able to provide value to the team or the project should be your goal.

Barreling into every situation and playing the same role is one of the leading examples of hubris in the workplace. It's like bringing a crescent wrench to a hammer party; instead of seeing your mistake and going home to get your hammer, you spend the evening bending nails. Instead, you should be carrying a big tool belt, wherever you go.

The Servant-Leader concept is a powerful one for a firm's marketing support staff. They are often at Ground Zero during the production of a proposal or interview. Junior staff members often approach these situations in a "reactionary" style—"just tell me what you want and I'll get it for you." As they develop in their careers, however, they are asked to facilitate or manage the pursuit process. Shifting from reactive to proactive, while still maintaining a position of support, means alternating from serving to leading to serving again, often within the space of a few minutes.

This is where great marketing people are born. In the white-hot crucible of a deadline driven pursuit, working with teams of eccentric personalities, differing communication styles, and opposing agendas. Great marketers can build relationships of trust, value, and common interest to move people toward a goal. It all starts with making a connection with another person. Business Development, like art, isn't a role, it's an action. Success is about performing the actions that define the role.

Behavioral Styles

It is important to appreciate the significance of behavioral styles in communicating with and selling to people. Behavioral styles differentiate personality traits, social characteristics, communication styles, and decision-making tendencies. These styles are important to business developers because they determine how a person will respond in a particular situation, and how they "make sense" of the world.

The Greek philosopher Hippocrates wrote about behavioral styles as far back as 400 BC. He described four "humours" or bodily fluids—Choleric, Sanguine, Melancholy and Phlegmatic—that were linked to types of temperaments. Karl Jung popularized the study of behavior in the early 1900s, and the topic has been extended by many others including David W. Merrill and Roger H. Reid[7], who adapted this knowledge to performance and decision-making in work settings. Any Google search of Behavioral Styles will bring forth a multitude of variations of the same four temperaments, described in many different ways, but essentially the same. These four behavioral styles can best be described with the words that have been associated with them by the many academics and authors that have published on this topic[8].

The first type is variously described as Director, Driver, Dominant, Can-Do, or simply as a D-style. As the words denote, people with this behavioral style can be decisive and independent, often making them the Alpha of a group. Though we're not advocating for one person's system, for this book, let's agree that the word Driver encompasses this style.

The second type is known by the words Thinker, Analytical, Compliance Style, Conscientiousness, and Perfectionist. We believe the lion's share of technical professionals have one foot in this category. By nature, technical professionals are drawn to the profession because of their ability to make important (in the case of bridge or elevator designers, life-and-death) decisions, based on the cold analysis of mountains of data. Let's settle on Analytical to describe this type of behavior.

The third type is known by the words Relater, Amiable, Steady, or S-style, which paint a picture of someone who seeks to get along with other people, values the status quo, is apprehensive of change, and who often seeks consensus within groups. Amiable is a good name for this type of behavior.

The fourth type is known as Socializer, Influencer, Expressive, or Talker. It would not be an exaggeration to contend that the vast majority of marketers are within this category, putting them in a separate camp from the technical people they serve. This is often why sales and technical teams can struggle to communicate; they often communicate in different

---

[7] Merrill, David W., and Roger H. Reid. Personal Styles and Effective Performance: Make Your Style Work for You. Radnor, PA: Chilton Book, 1981

[8] The Effectiveness Institute of Redmond, WA uses terms Analyzer, Controller, Stabilizer, Persuader, as examples of the dozens of terms often used to describe behavioral states.

ways, and frequently they can all be found talking at once. The key, therefore, in communicating effectively is to understand the style of the person with whom you are attempting to communicate and make sure you give them the information they need to make a decision.

The four basic types are often depicted in a matrix, or diagrammatically. Obviously, describing a person's personality in one word is an oversimplification, but a simple model is helpful in understanding and relating to people. More importantly, the model can offer insights into means of appealing to each personality type to make a persuasive argument. Rather than falling readily into one of the four styles, people tend to behave in a combination of styles, one of which is dominant. Most of the time, those styles are adjacent to each other on the diagram. For example, someone who is an *Analytical*-Amiable tends most heavily toward data-driven decisions, but can compromise within groups in order to gain consensus.

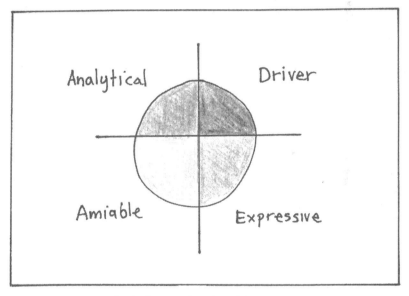

Determining the behavioral style of decision-makers is a process of asking questions and talking to them over a period of time in a way that reveals characteristics. Though we would not request it of a client, we often complete a questionnaire to illustrate the process. There are many proprietary questionnaires on the internet which ask between 30-50 questions, the answers placing you into a category.

When you first participate in this type of activity, you may be skeptical. But over the years we have seen hundreds of people perform this exercise, and it always raises awareness. Activities that elicit discussion of how to effectively communicate with people are rarely a waste of time.

We have been surveyed many times using many of the copyrighted methods that have been developed. Using the names we have settled on in this chapter, Harold is considered to be a *Driver*-Expressive, a blend of styles, though tilting toward Driver. Charles has been defined as an *Expressive*-Amiable. Since we have different predominant styles, but both share a style, we believe this makes us complementary. Two Drivers in a partnership would constantly argue; two Amiables would never get anything decided.

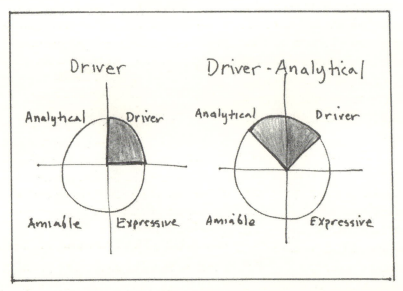

No matter the name of the style, three things are important to remember:
1) All people have a dominant way in which they interpret what they hear and how they speak.
2) It is critical that you identify your own communication style AND the style of the person with whom you are attempting to communicate.
3) It is YOUR responsibility to communicate effectively to persuade the person with whom you are speaking.

Clients, fellow employees, or team partners all have tendencies to communicate and make decisions in a certain way. The only way to bond with someone is to effectively adjust to their communication style and continuously monitor that they are hearing what you intend to convey. The distance between your mouth and their ears can sometimes be miles apart.

Adaptive Selling

Pioneering work has been done by Barton Weitz[9][10] and co-authors on the importance of behavioral styles to the interpersonal interactions of people in sales situations, which is where the study topic provides real value. And this topic is especially important when discussing selling to complex groups of people on selection committees.

Adaptive selling is a process in which business developers tailor their communication and competitive strategies based on the style of the client, hand-in-hand with an understanding of their own personality style. This is common sense, as most of us subconsciously adjust our communication to the people we are talking to. Many business developers barrel into clients' offices and start in on the "pitch" they have spent hours developing. This is often ineffective, not because of the pitch, but because it is not communicated in a manner in which the listener wants to hear it.

> The topic of adjusting communication styles is best illustrated by the relationship I have with one of my company's leading technical engineers. I often drive him nuts.
>
> When I announced at a meeting once that we won a million dollar contract, my intention was to get our team excited about a new sale. But my friend raised his hand and asked, "wasn't it an $820,000 contract?" Well, yes, but isn't that close enough to a million? Not to him.
>
> It doesn't matter what I intend; what matters is how my message is received. If my intention was to get him excited about a sale, then I should have adjusted my description of the sale to obtain the effect. That's if a $820,000 contract really excites him.

We are not talking about ways to "manipulate" clients, rather in adjusting your communication to their style for maximum effectiveness. At first blush, many technical professionals recoil at this technique, with the knee-jerk reaction that it is "selfishly salesy." We see it differently. By

---

[9] Weitz, Barton A. "Effectiveness in Sales Interactions: A Contingency Framework." Journal of Marketing 45.1 (1981): 85

[10] Weitz, Barton A., Harish Sujan, and Mita Sujan. "Knowledge, Motivation, and Adaptive Behavior: A Framework for Improving Selling Effectiveness." Journal of Marketing 50.4 (1986): 174.

adjusting communication styles to that of the client, we are making the ultimate adaption to their needs in the interest of solving their problem. The following comments may convince you of the value of this topic.

Driver
- From a sales standpoint, Drivers tend to place less importance on personal relationships ("Just gimme the facts"), so spend less time trying to become a buddy.
- Always ask questions to break the ice. This allows them to take the lead, and do not interrupt them.
- Be brief; get to the bottom line quickly. Focus on cost-related benefits that can be proven by credible evidence. Present alternatives, rather than telling them what is best for them. They want to make the decision; you might be surprised how quickly this occurs.
- When making a presentation to them, go easy on the visual aids; they can be a distraction from the bottom line. Invite questions. You may need to start with the answer and work backwards.
- Expect to be challenged, but be cautious in challenging back. You might be tested to see how you respond.

For Amiables and Expressives, talking to Drivers is not as challenging as you might think. We like to listen and we like to ask questions. Drivers love to talk and they love to teach. Some styles are naturally complementary. However, sending your Driver CEO into a meeting with a Driver client General Manager will take some extra coaching by the sales team to make sure they don't crash into each other.

Analytical
- Be prepared; do your homework. Understand the client's business as thoroughly as you can before meeting. Advanced research will be worth the effort.
- Get your facts right. Emphasize proven results and well-documented features of your services. Be sure to note the advantages and disadvantages of your approach or concept. Rely on tables, graphs, and written documents that you can leave for them to study in detail afterward. Don't be shy about using numbers in your arguments or proofs. They will proofread your proposals, qualifications, and anything else you give them.

- Use logic and reason; avoid giving your own opinion. Stay low-key, and avoid theatrics or emotions – these will get you nowhere and may damage your cause.

For Amiables and Expressives, talking to Analyticals can be the most challenging (see sidebar). We tend not to worry about the exactness of the data we're presenting or the details of the design, but rather the "overall impression." This is why artists and accountants often are at odds.

Amiable

- Avoid moving directly to the main issue. Your first objective is to demonstrate authenticity and your humanistic side. They must believe you have their best interest in mind. Get to a first-name basis as quickly as comfortable.
- For the long haul, invest time in developing a personal relationship. This will serve you both well, as you work toward win-win solutions.
- Approach solutions with personal information. Generic approaches will not work, because they are not personalized. Work on understanding their feelings and be empathetic.
- Offer personal assurances, not warrantees. Prepare personal references and case histories, along with individuals to contact.

Throwing a Party

A convenient way to remember each of the personality characteristics is to consider the role each type might play in throwing a party.

The **Driver** will abruptly announce that there is a need for a party, and that it be held this evening. He or she will likely appoint someone to be in charge.

Analyticals get busy developing checklists, including an invitation list. They start thinking about the venue, and the food and drink to be served. They call the caterer, buy party favors, and worry about the logistics of parking.

The **Expressive** stands at the entrance to the party, tie loosened, greeting guests with hugs. Eventually, they may end up with a lamp shade on their head.

The **Amiable** scurries around making sure everyone is having a good time. They ask if everyone has had enough to drink or if the room seems too warm or cold. At the end of the party, they may not have actually eaten or drank anything.

Amiables want to know which of their friends have selected you for a project. They have a large network of contacts in their industry and they base many decisions a personal level. So, connecting your network to theirs is a good way to gain credibility.

Expressive

- Focus on helping them with their personal goals, in addition to achieving benefits for their organization. Ask them about their hopes and dreams for the project you're discussing, as well as their greatest fears. Your ultimate goal is reaching a shared vision.
- Ask open-ended questions, then sit back and listen. Let them talk. Feel free to use some showmanship in presenting big picture concepts. You may be surprised at how animated they become in response.
- Under no circumstances should you argue with them (whereas Analyticals love a good argument). This will do no good. Instead, suggest an alternative vision or plant the seeds of a broad new dream.
- Acknowledge their intelligence and vision. Flattery and positive assurances work with them.

Expressives often talk in stories and anecdotes. They are the best dinner speakers at your company retreats, because they have a natural ability to tap into the emotions of a room. If this describes employees, maximize their behavior by allowing them to be the "cheerleaders" of your organization.

In our experience, the best approach for applying adaptive selling techniques to a complex organization is to look at the client's team, then diagnose each relevant position against the four-behavioral styles. These can be shown graphically on an organization chart, using the symbols expressed to the right of each box.

When you walk into a company's War Room, where people are busy preparing for a multi-million dollar sale, this type of charting is a sign that they are seriously interested in delivering their message in the most effective way. The moment of truth in marketing is getting the customer to say "Yes." For a competition that is anticipated to be hotly competed, then it is important to pull out all of the stops and pay attention to detail, because every little thing matters.

We are often asked about the perception that building relationships with the intention of developing business can seem shallow or even fake. Indeed, we've seen more than our share of these cases. However, we can also testify that the vast majority of professional relationships are founded in trust, respect, and mutual benefit. Clients need relationships with us, as much as we need ones with them. We think the checks and balances of human behavior are perfectly efficient at ferreting out impostors, and so our best advice is to stop worrying about seeming to be mercenary and let nature take its course.

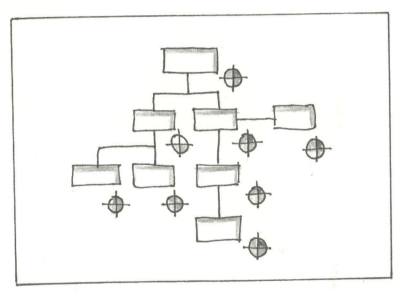

Is it possible to win new work with a new client without the benefit of relationships? Absolutely. It's done all the time. It all depends on the strength of your technology or the range of your price. However, another firm could easily overcome your edge, simply by playing the relationship trump card.

You Already Have Working Relationships

Unless you are starting your career from scratch, you are already working with a variety of clients and teaming partners. Normally, if you and your firm are performing well, you are already building productive relationships. This is quite natural, and will happen without thinking very much about it. They may be solid enough to reward your firm with repeat business, one of the most highly sought-after positions. Over time, a series of repeat assignments will inevitably foster stronger relationships, founded in mutual respect and trust.

The Value of Relationships When Problems Occur

Projects often experience challenges. These commonly arise and can be difficult to overcome under the best of circumstances. A secure relationship between the technical professional and customer can be a key ingredient to resolving the stickiest problems. If you're thinking that a customer will cut you some slack when there is a problem, think again. Realistically, a strong relationship helps both parties to weather tough times, based on a foundation of trust and respect. Relationships help both parties to empathize with one another's situation, shift the attention to solutions, and to move on. A positive outcome after resolution of a problem has the added benefit of building goodwill and strengthening the relationship.

Provided you do not need to compete for work to grow your practice, you could survive nicely off the relationships formed naturally over time. However, if you compete for work, then you can't afford to wait forever for relationships to form. You must make a concerted, planned effort to get to know new clients, and accelerate the process of forming positive relationships.

Tips for Building Relationships

Here are some tips which we have found helpful in initiating and cultivating relationships, especially with those individuals with whom you find it difficult to get to know:

- Obviously, nothing works as well as setting up an appointment for a good old fashioned face-to-face meeting. Sounds simple, but many technical professionals ASSUME clients don't want to meet with them. We cannot tell you how many times we hear, "I don't want to bug them." You won't bug them, if you provide value.
- If someone more senior in your firm, or a teaming partner, has a relationship with a client, then tag along. It is in the best interest of a colleague or partner to expand the number of connections to a client. It takes the pressure off of a cold call. It also helps shy staff members to survive the initial few minutes of small talk, and allows someone else to handle the introductions.

- Try to place yourself in the same location, at the same time, with the client. This is the major value of conferences, although chance encounters in large venues are hard to pull off. Professional committee work is better for getting to know people; working hard and contributing in a committee is one way to prove yourself to the targeted individual. In selecting conferences and committees, do your homework and select the right ones.
- Be realistic. A 24-year-old junior engineer is unlikely to be able to attain the status of trusted advisor to a 60-something general manager. While some might consider age to be an unfair barrier, the fact of the matter is that young staff will not have gained relevant professional experience of much value to the general manager. It would even be difficult to find common ground on social topics, given the generational difference.
- Look for ways of providing value, especially early on, but don't expect anything in return. Sending over a journal article, portion of a report, or other useful item helps cement an initial meeting into memory. Also, send a hand-written note of thanks for the person's time. A personal note is somewhat lost in this age of e-mail and text messages, but its rarity means that it can have a big impact.
- Select clients you think you might like, and for which you have shared values. Although this seems obvious, you'll be more successful in developing relationships if there is chemistry. Knowing who you will NOT call on is valuable because it keeps you from wasting energy. At the same time, you cannot ignore important clients where there may not be an immediate personal fit. We advise gritting your teeth and doing the best that you can. Experience shows that if you're sincere, a relationship will develop over time that benefits both parties.
- Be sure to allow a new acquaintance to control the flow of the conversation. Talk about what they want to talk about. How will you know this? Through active listening, it won't be long before you have ample ammunition to pick up on their interests. By asking clarifying questions, you'll quickly learn even more about their issues and challenges. It also doesn't hurt to prepare by doing a little research through the internet or networking with others who may know the client. If you're an "Expressive," you may find it

hard to resist the urge to talk about yourself. But resist, apply discipline and self-control, or your efforts will not be productive.
- Also resist the urge to give advice early on. You'll be asked soon enough. Technical professionals compulsively offer advice, sometimes in the first minute of an introduction! Although you may have the best of intentions, offering early advice can be negatively received because it is audacious to suggest a solution to someone who has invested time in wrestling with an issue and you have not.
- Know when to give up – to know me is not *necessarily* to love me. You won't be able to hit it off with everyone, and so you must become adept at reading the signs that a relationship is either not going to form, or will level off at a low plateau. This can be hard to accept, but is something you must watch for. On the positive side, there are more people in the world than you can possibly know; move on.
- In international settings, American technical professionals need to keep cultural rules in mind. We have a tendency to get straight to business in meetings. Outside of the United States, business is more often conducted on the strength of relationships, with parties needing to get to know one another first. Much to the chagrin of most Yankees, serious business decisions are not going to be made until a bond is formed. Patience is the operative advice, if working off-shore.
- Relationships require maintenance. A good colleague once advised to "never throw away your little black book." Letting a relationship go stale that you have invested time and money in is an unfortunate waste. A diligent effort to stay in touch takes a minimal effort and is worthwhile. If you have lost touch, don't be too embarrassed to call; reconnect and get things moving again.

Relationships with Top Management

An important question is how broad of a relationship with a client organization is needed to be comfortable? A lot depends on who is making hiring decisions at the client organization. You probably don't need to be golfing buddies with the General Manager, if he/she isn't involved in selection processes or decisions that impact your firm. On the other hand, it would be wise if he/she knew your name, and that of your firm. We've often said that upper echelon people in your client organization should know enough about your company to be able to defend it in your absence. One example might be the case of a contract renewal before a City Council meeting. If the decision to award was being challenged for political reasons, and the General Manager could deal with the issue on the spot, your odds of surviving the challenge are much more likely than if the controversy were to drag on to a future meeting.

It's a simple fact that many individuals within a client's organization may not make themselves available to you, for whatever reason. Sometimes, highly placed executives don't want to be bothered with technical professionals calling on them. If you're marketing to a Fortune 1000 company, chances are that the CEO is not going to find time to meet with you. Your client analysis and capture plan should identify the individuals with whom you should try to make contact. If there are certain members of upper management who are deemed important for your firm, then you may need to try an alternative approach to get close to them.

Assessing Relationship Strength

One of the most important skills that a marketer can develop is the ability to assess the strength of a relationship. Most people (especially technical professionals with large egos) overestimate the depth of their relationship with a client. To make this even more difficult, management and marketing support staff may never meet the client, which means they have to trust others to assure that the "base is covered."

The best way to assess relationship strength is to personally observe it. If you're a marketer, this will be difficult to arrange because you won't get invited to project meetings. However, if you are able to attend client entertainment functions or participate in committees, these events may be good opportunities. We've known marketers who have a remarkable ability to assess the relationship of a client and a technical professional by watching from across a crowded room, simply by reading body language.

It's important for marketers to remember that they can have valuable relationships with existing clients. Clear it with the manager first, but you can make a "wellness" check with a client. Say to the client, "Our PM has the project uppermost in his mind. I'm most interested in how we're doing as a firm. We value your business and want to keep working with you on future projects." Keep the meeting brief and report the results back to the PM. In this manner, the marketer provides confirmation of the client/firm relationship. Clients typically appreciate the "check-in" from someone who is not active on the project.

If you're not able to see the interaction between the technical professional and client, quiz the technical professional about the nature of his/her relationship with the client. We often see marketers or management get trapped in allowing technical professionals to rate their own relationships. The only way you're going to be able to validate is to ask probing questions about the relationship, such as:
- How long they have known one another?
- Have they attended social functions together?
- What do you know about the client's personal life (e.g., hobbies)?
- How has the relationship come into play during a selection?
- For projects, have you been through tough times together?

The second mode of assessing relationship strength is to triangulate. Talk to others in the firm, and anyone else you can find, to get a reality-check on the relationship. Clients for whom your firm has a long history of work, and in which other technical professionals are involved, are a good source of corroboration. We suggest you be judicious about this—many colleagues won't reveal negatives during a pursuit meeting in front of others. You may need to do some office-hopping with the door shut before there is comfort in disclosing a differing assessment.

Listen for indicators that reveal the strength of your competition's relationships with clients. In our experience, trying to determine the strength of the competition is even harder to do than for that of your own firm because there are fewer sources with whom you can triangulate. Over time, you can learn to listen for the competition's experience, project activities and other social and entertainment events, as well. Be aware of who else is doing work for the client. Keep an ear to the ground, especially for successes and failures which can offer insights into the competition's strengths and weaknesses. This information will be key in developing a strategy for differentiating yourself from your competition.

Avoiding Pitfalls

On the topic of developing relationships, there are some specific pitfalls to be avoided:
- Relationships, like construction projects, are not built in a day. Do not become a stalker. It's easy to overdo it, especially when an upcoming pursuit is on the line. If you're not careful, you can be-

come viewed as a pest. This is shooting yourself in the foot. Go slow and look for signs of reciprocation to avoid this trap.
- Don't boast or tell white lies. This should go without saying, but we've seen it happen. There's a lot to be gained from staying humble, and having humility on your side. One little lie, or half-truth, and you may be damaged forever. Worse yet, your poor reputation will spread, and it will damage your efforts with other clients (and likely your own colleagues).
- Good news travels fast, bad news travels at light speed. If your firm makes a mistake or gets bad press, be sure to reveal the information to clients with whom you're trying to build a relationship. It'll be better coming from you, as you're representing your firm, than from your competition.
- Keep it platonic. We've seen technical professionals develop personal relationships that lead to dating, significant other-ship, and more. Our best advice is, don't. We suppose sometimes these things can't be helped, but nine times out of ten they end badly. They create a perception of the ultimate conflict of interest, and often damage both parties in the eyes of their colleagues.
- Don't try to be all things to all people. In an age of specialization, the client knows you can't be an expert on more than a few topics. Tell the client you don't know the answer, then schedule a meeting to bring the subject matter experts with you to discuss complicated issues. In the end you'll be respected, and the client will gain an appreciation for the depth of your firm's capabilities.
- Heighten your sensitivity to the competition. Do they periodically meet with you to discuss teaming opportunities? Assume the worst– that they are using you to perform their own triangulation of your positioning with the client. If the teaming discussions never lead to anything, then they may be using you.
- Never cross into territory that is illegal, unethical, or immoral. Many of the rules, policies, or laws which apply to procurements are in place for good reasons. You would be well advised to become cognizant of them because what makes your client look bad will also drag you down. One of our favorite tests is to consider how an idea, event, or gift will look on the front page of your local paper. If it doesn't smell right, then it probably isn't, and is not worth it.

If You're a Client

If you're reading this book as a client, the relationships you form with your service providers are critical to the success of your project. Relationships are as important to clients as to technical professionals. You have a lot to gain by understanding the highly competitive nature of the marketplace, and the approaches taken by firms to win your work.

If you're on the alert, then you can become aware of superficial or disingenuous approaches. A service-provider who believes in a strong relationship with you will work harder to solve your problems. At the same time, we caution you to be objective. Know when your service provider is being sincere and when they are not. Only the test of time will validate mutual respect and trust. Be mindful of your decisions and your inherent bias in selecting your buddy rather than the most qualified firm. You'll be doing yourself and your organization a big favor in making a good choice.

> *The dilemma over whether to "go around" our client and talk to the people at the political level of the organization was hotly debated. Proponents argued that if the competition were doing it, then we needed to level the playing field. Opponents countered that it wouldn't be worth it, because of the potential for the tactic to backfire. They noted that politicians come and go, but staff is employed forever.*
>
> *In the end, we decided not to go political. Staff members were undergoing changes and the transition placed an old friend in a new management role. We decided to contact the new manager and make it clear that we would not go over his head to the politicians.*
>
> *And sure enough, we were not selected. A Monday-morning quarterback might critique this decision. However, looking back, we made the right choice. During the telephone conversation with the manager, after I explained that we would not be playing the politics card, his response was, "Thanks. This really means a lot to me." Over the years there have been many other opportunities, some won, and some lost. But we maintained a great relationship of which we were proud.*

Chapter 3
Competitive Strategies for Winning Pursuits

"Shallow men believe in luck. Strong men believe in cause and effect."
- Ralph Waldo Emerson

We faced a dilemma: an RFP arrived on our doorstep for the design of a large project. The client was a city in the American heartland with whom we had not been successful on two recent pursuits. We felt that we had done our homework in the prior two pursuits, but placed an agonizing second both times to the same firm. We had no appetite for a third losing effort.

The project location was a challenge because our company did not have an office in the state. Our previous strategy to address this weakness was to partner with a local firm. However, we discovered that our past teaming partner was not as respected by the client as we originally thought.

A third challenge was the need for a project manager who would agree to move to the City during design and construction. Of the suitable candidates from around the firm, one man was enthusiastic and was willing to move, but lacked experience in similarly-sized projects.

After talking to the client and receiving assurance that the procurement was "wide open", technical staff wanted to submit a proposal. Management wasn't so sure. We desperately needed a strategy.

The Importance of a Competitive Strategy

Our definition of a strategy is a careful plan or method for achieving a specific goal or result. Strategy is relevant to many areas of life, from getting the right date for the school prom to running a business. For example, the goal of a company may be to increase profits: the strategy chosen might be to undertake an advertising campaign; invest in a new computer system; or adjust pricing. When it comes to winning projects for technical services, we have seen a superior strategy allow a small, 2-person firm win a contract over a corporation with 30,000 employees. They understood that formulating, refining, and then delivering a sales strategy could level the playing field.

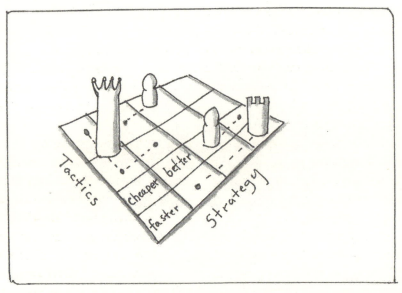

Because of the universal importance of strategy in achieving success, we see it applied everywhere-- chess, sports, business, and the military. There are even published texts on how to relate to your teenager by applying parenting strategies.

Before drilling down into this topic, we would be remiss if we did not emphasize the importance of leadership and timing in the development of sales strategies. Leadership drives action; specifically, leadership drives a team to be proactive. *The earlier you formulate a competitive strategy, the faster you can direct your firm's positioning activities*. Starting early to develop a competitive strategy is a cornerstone to positioning. We repeatedly see teams brainstorming the technical aspects of a pursuit, developing brilliant solutions, but paying almost no attention on formulating a competitive strategy. It's an example of technical professionals following their instinct to apply systematic reasoning to develop solutions to tangible problems. Great for building bridges, but not for probing into the psyches of selection committees.

Unfortunately, most technical activities are tactical, not strategic. A "big idea" can be a game changer in meeting the client's unmet need, but the calculations, selection of equipment, drafting of drawings, and other work is almost all tactical. This underscores the importance of going beyond the technical work, and getting to the art (or emotional side) of decision-making. The rocket scientists in your firm may resist this. In their minds, the client's perfect solution must lay somewhere under all those details. Left unchecked, they will spend all their available marketing time (indeed stay up all night) in search of the technical silver bullet.

As a result, marketing staff are left to cobble together a strategy at the eleventh hour, in the heat of proposal production. Still worse, we've seen many proposals with no competitive strategy whatsoever. It is very difficult to be successful if this is your approach.

Regardless, if your background is technical or marketing, do not wait to be told what to do. Take the lead! If you're a marketing coordinator, facilitate a discussion on how to win the pursuit. We make a strong case that this is a primary responsibility of marketing professionals, as a means of creating value in their position. Our advice is to have a bias for action and tackle the difficult issues first because the easy ones can wait. Focus on overcoming your weaknesses and uncovering the information you know you don't know, as well as the information you don't know you don't know. Proactive leadership of this type is highly valued and often rewarded.

Characteristics of Competitive Strategies

A competitive strategy is the core reason why the client should select your company for an assignment. If you find yourself unable to clearly and easily state this for an impending procurement, then how would you expect a client to be able to? As an example, let's assume that the Jones Consulting team is proposing

> A competitive strategy should:
> 1. Address the client's unmet needs
> 2. Be simple and emotional
> 3. Differentiate you from your competitors by being cheaper, better, faster
> 4. Be proven
> 5. Contain tactics that can be implemented
> 6. Interlink with related strategies
> 7. Reduce risk through relationships
> 8. Sell to your strengths

to help a City expand its vehicle maintenance facility. Their strategy to win this lucrative contract may sound something like this: "The Jones

Consulting team's design concept to efficiently rebuild the proposed facility, instead of replacing it, will save millions in construction costs and reduce its footprint."

A persuasive strategy such as the example above may seem simple on its surface, but can sometimes take months or years to develop. Because of the abstract nature of this topic (a major reason why technical professionals struggle with it), discussing the characteristics of good competitive strategies is helpful:

1) First and foremost, **competitive strategies should address the client's unmet needs**. This means investing a considerable amount of time in listening to the client. The conversations are meant not to determine what the project involves, but what problem the project is intended to solve. If you don't know why the client is performing the project, you'll never discover a solution that satisfies them.

While this is easy to say, it can become quite complicated. The client is often more than one individual; the winning decision may be in the hands of a committee. Each member may have different expectations for the project. You may need to orchestrate a complex response to multiple, varied needs, some of which may be contradictory. For example, Jones Consulting may have discovered that a two-person committee will be responsible for selecting a consultant for its vehicle maintenance facility upgrade. One person is looking for a team that will provide the least costly solution. The other member is most interested in a solution that won't cause complaints from neighboring homeowners. These two seemingly disconnected needs could be met with a single solution for the project that minimizes the costs to construct, while also making it more com-

> *When asked by reporters how he felt about his son not winning the Presidency of the United States by a majority of the popular vote, Joseph Kennedy responded, "I'll be damned if I'm going to finance a landslide."*
>
> *From a marketer's point of view, this makes a lot of sense. We often see technical professionals scrambling to run calculations, develop concepts, prepare graphics, even prepare full-blown designs in support of proposals. What if some of their effort – or all of it – wasn't relevant to the competitive strategy? Then it's a waste of precious time and money.*
>
> *While we are not advocating winning by the narrowest of margins, JFK's dad had a point. If you develop your competitive strategy early, then your team can avoid unnecessary activities which don't enhance the strategy.*

pact, allowing more "buffer" from neighboring homeowners.

2) The essence of a competitive strategy should be simple and emotional, rather than technical. Ideally, the best strategy can be understood quickly by people who do not possess the years of schooling and experience of the technical professional. A strategy may be based on discrete criteria, such as low cost or superior technology, but the reason the project is important to a decision-maker is probably based on an emotional need, rather than a technical one. This is especially true when a selection committee includes a non-technical member, such as a city councilperson, who may be more heavily influenced by the perception of their constituents, rather than the details of a particular technology. We've often said that you should be able to explain your strategy for winning a $100 million project to your mother during a 60-second elevator ride.

> Our favorite people in our industry are those that enjoy developing strategies for winning new work. They naturally are interested in identifying value for the client. They are the type of people who walk into a strategy session and say, "OK people, let's save the client some money."
>
> That statement gets the team thinking about providing value to the client, new ways of looking at the technical challenges of the project, and ideas that differentiate the team from the competition. The results: clients select them for their work.
>
> Hats off to the strategists.

An example: the solution you propose for a pursuit is an architecturally complex administrative building placed on a site that you propose the client purchase through a six-way property transfer using foreign derivatives. Yahoo, you're a genius. But, your competitor proposes a simple building based on the log cabin built by the first settlers to the region. They understand that the most influential decision-maker is a fourth generation resident of the community and has been searching for an opportunity to leave a historic legacy to his community. The competitor wins the job. The only way to discover the unmet needs of your clients is to ask them, then ask them again.

3) Competitive strategies are frequently rooted in the axiom: cheaper, better, faster. A strategy that plays to an emotionally-based need will be stronger if it is linked to a quantitative advantage that separates your solution from any other. Solutions that quantify an advantage to the client create a differentiator from your competitors. Thinking in terms of superlatives (good, better, best) supports the ranking of your solution in the top of the client's mind.

For example, you may be considering a strategy that proposes to shorten the construction schedule of the client's project. You have identified that a faster schedule will meet your client's unmet need (meeting the first characteristic), and appeal to his emotional desire to show his bosses that he can "get things done" (the second characteristic). Reducing the schedule 30% by pre-purchasing equipment (if it's realistic for the technical team) is quantifiably "faster" and sets the bar for the competition.

4) Effective competitive strategies are supported with proof. Nothing validates a sales pitch as much as a verifiable example of having provided a similar solution for another respected client. Everyone is comforted to know that the challenges they face are not unique. When you link your strategy to an example of "Where you've done it before," you are doing the one thing that can counter a lack of a relationship with a client. You are saying, "If the client down the road trusts us, then maybe you should, too." Current, relevant proof of success (with testimonials from your clients) will greatly improve the impact of your strategy.

Now, we have all seen firms win projects for service that they had never before performed. There's always a first for every firm— your first five-story masonry building, your first project in the State of Texas, your first financial services contract using a new computer program. You don't necessarily have to show-off an exact replica of the proposed project, but you have to make a critical connection between your past experience and your aspirations. And those connections don't have to relate to size, color, or construction material. Rather, your strategy can connect to core values shared by the owners of the two projects. Perhaps the project you provide as proof is half as large as the one you are seeking to win, but they had similarly tight schedule requirements (the shared driver of the two clients).

5) Competitive strategies must lead to tactics that can be implemented. This may overstate the obvious, but the greatest competitive strategy in the world is worthless if you and your firm can't implement the supporting tactics. So, in formulating strategies, it is important to work within the confines of your capabilities. Does this mean you shouldn't think out of the box? Absolutely not. Expanding your box is important if you want to grow into new markets and services.

Strategies for addressing a shortfall include innovating your processes or technology, or teaming with other firms to combine skill sets. If your strategy is to build an anti-gravity device or partner with the New York Yankees, then you better be able to deliver, because it's hollow and unworkable if the tactics aren't actionable.

6) Strategies are commonly interlinked. The easiest (and perhaps oldest) demonstration of a linked strategy is the adage that time is money. If the deadline is important to your client, and you can identify an approach which meets or beats the schedule, then your strategy may have a secondary benefit beyond saving time, saving money. Keep in mind that it is not always that simple; accelerating a schedule can also drive up costs or create collateral risks. Almost all actions can have unexpected consequences. But they also have unexpected benefits that compound the value to the client. These take time to develop. But this is a topic that technical staff members often engage with because of the logical piecing together of ideas, a process much like working on a project.

Another example of interlinked strategies is in the application of innovative ideas or technologies. Although it is common for the initial investment in a new technical solution to be higher, a business case can be made that there will be long range cost savings or other elusive benefits. These benefits might include greater control, improved customer service, or enhanced safety. A team that invests time into discussing strategy will be rewarded with a brainstorm of ideas that develop into ancillary benefits to the client. A new construction method, for example, that is not only less expensive, but also results in fewer permits, which accelerates the schedule, which completes the project before the election, which helps the politician's campaign may be the "killer" strategy that wins you the job. Chess players who are master strategists can see ahead to more moves than their opponents. The ability to anticipate, react, counter, and rethink is the primary tool of the strategist.

7) Relationships are often at the core of competitive strategies. If you have developed a strong relationship with a client over time, (perhaps you're even considered a trusted advisor), the strength of this bond can be a powerful element in your competitive strategy. It is important to keep in mind that many projects with technical services firms require change. For many people, change means risk. A relationship of trust allays the fear of that risk. Minimizing risk is a fundamental strategy that trumps just about everything (hence, the value of being an incumbent). It can be difficult to overcome the strength of a competitor's relationship. This is one of the main reasons for investing time to position for opportunities well in advance of the release of the procurement documents to allow relationships to be formed.

8) Sell to your strengths. Lastly, it is wise to avoid flimsy or weak rationale. This is easier said than done and, like a lot of things, it is often more clear in hindsight. In our experience, selling to your strengths tends to be a concept reached through an iterative process of testing and re-testing. A good example would be proposing a project manager from a local office who has only a few years of experience, rather than a senior staff member with better qualifications from a distant office. The client has said that local knowledge is important, so the team's strategy is addressing a known hot button. However, a stronger strategy may be to propose the more experienced project manager, with the local staff person as a deputy. Playing to your strengths sometimes means taking calculated risks, but typically erring toward the strategy that you know will result in the better project.

Formulating Competitive Strategies

Frequently, when faced with developing a strategy, one of the greatest challenges is getting started. As systematic as technical professionals can be in solving problems, their approach to marketing and sales can be quite the opposite. Many technical professionals are blind to the methodology of forming strategies to win new work.

If lightning strikes and marketing, business development, and technical staff find themselves in a room to figure out how to win a project, there are several methods for structuring the conversation to develop a competitive strategy. First, you should be brainstorming with the entire pursuit team. This solidifies buy-in. There is nothing worse than a teammate who does not believe in the strategy of a pursuit because they will never be believable in an interview with the client. It's also important to appreciate that marketers selling their own competitive strategies, without support of the technical professional staff, will ultimately fail. The best example of this is the salesperson who consistently underprices proposals, or makes promises that are difficult to keep, such as unrealistic deadlines. Sales pitches without the support of those who will be doing the work are rarely sustainable.

1) Focus on the results. You can't fully understand a client's issues unless you think about solutions. A worthwhile early activity is to "fast-forward" to conclusions and explore alternatives. By fully examining the potential solutions, the major issues will be identified. However, it is important to maintain an open mind – technical people have a tendency to jump to conclusions and be reluctant to explore alternatives. A sensitivity analysis that slightly varies possible solutions can explore "what if?" scenarios. This helps to surface pros and cons, which compare and contrast different aspects of the project.

> *Formulating a competitive strategy involves asking your team to:*
> 1. *Focus on the results*
> 2. *Brainstorm the process*
> 3. *Compare/contrast to the competition*
> 4. *Get smarter*
> 5. *Provide better people*
> 6. *Build the perfect beast*

In almost all cases, the cost of a project is a significant issue. It is not too early during initial discussions to begin developing costs, whether for the fees for your services, or the client's total cost for the final project. Because of the importance of cost, this topic should be revisited frequently over the life of the pursuit, as your solutions are refined.

A good facilitator is needed to keep this process from going astray. Rules of thumb:

- Don't allow strong personalities to overwhelm the brainstorming process. Just because an idea is presented more loudly than another, doesn't make it more valid.
- Be prepared for high level people on your team to say, "We can't draw any conclusions, we don't have enough information about the project." A proper response is, "Then let's gather more information. But we'll need to perform this process soon; I'm sure our competitors are."
- Place a time limit on this endeavor. This is typically an activity that the technical team enjoys; they are often reluctant to halt this process and move to other aspects of developing a strategy.

Lastly, a focus on technical results will also allow you to begin to evaluate your project team, how they reach conclusions, their interaction, how they cope with challenges, and how they might perform in client interviews. Use this process to winnow underperformers, or unproductive internal relationships.

2) Brainstorm the process. Most projects are not solely focused on the end result; the process of reaching the result is also critically important. There's a reason that many clients ask for your "approach" to a project, not simply the cost. Consideration needs to be given to the sequence of events, as well as the elements and people providing input to the project. Schedules or flow charts are helpful to identify the key activities of an assignment along with their interrelationships. Other process-oriented tools include checklists of decision criteria or computer models for reaching decisions.

3) Compare/Contrast to the competition. Once your team has developed initial ideas and processes for developing solutions, you should compare them with others that most likely will be proposed by your competition, especially an incumbent. And there's nearly always an incumbent. Unless the client is newly incorporated, whose staff recently emigrated from Mars, there are existing relationships established by competitors that you will be compared to. Therefore, understand the marketplace, refine your ideas ruthlessly, and look for the superlatives— faster, better, cheaper.

4) Get smarter. This is actually a method of compensating for a weakness, filling in for a lack of know-how or experience. In this approach, you visit other clients who faced similar challenges. The goal is to learn as much as possible about approaches taken by others. If you include clients who've had work performed by competitors, you

> The best example we've seen of "getting smart" resulted in winning a significant procurement, while also ushering in a major new product line for the company. A municipality desired to develop a new water supply in response to population growth. The client planned to implement "program management" to supplement their staff capabilities.
>
> We grew concerned that our credentials in program management were weaker than the competition. We wanted to eliminate, or at least neutralize, this issue from the selection process.
>
> We devised a plan to survey other municipalities and compile a report on their program management experiences. Our Project Manager visited over 20 clients. The results were compiled in an easily-readable report, with tables for easy comparison of lessons learned.
>
> Our proposed Program Manager learned a lot and became a knowledgeable and confident candidate for the project.
>
> Our firm was selected for the work, and that report was updated many times for other pursuits.

can both increase your knowledge of the project's challenges, but also your competitors' likely strategies.

Most clients welcome these types of visits and enjoy sharing their experiences. You may be surprised at how candid they will be, not only about results that turned out well, but also about problems and failures. In a professional setting, you're clearly not going to inform a selection committee about a competitor's failures. However, if done carefully, a list of "lessons learned" is a compelling neutralizer.

5) Provide better people. Invest some time vetting your project team and organization, ensuring that all required areas of expertise are included, and that you have a management structure scaled to fit the size of the engagement.

For procurements that will likely lead to a presentation in front of the client, build your organization around your best interview team. (If you're a client, consider how many times you've turned down a firm because their proposed project manager lacked charisma at an interview, even though you knew he or she could do the job.) By identifying who will do well at the interview, and who might struggle, the project organization can be crafted around individual strengths and weaknesses.

6) Build the perfect beast. You may find that the most compelling strategy involves talent or technology that you do not possess. If necessary, you can team with other firms to access expertise you do not have. Specialty firms can be selected not only for their talents, but also for their relationships and political connections. We have been part of teams that were comprised of as many as 25 firms.

In addition, some people are fond of a strategy of reducing the number of competitors by teaming with some of them. Keep in mind that this technique may contribute to winning, but then your firm has to live with the shotgun marriage (and reduced revenue to your firm) when conducting the work. The team must benefit the client's project.

Take a dose of reality

After the team has stepped through this process, the resulting competitive strategy needs to be tested with cold eyes. Outsiders brought in to review your progress might identify a "blown read" or other misunderstanding of the client's needs. This is hard work. Many people would prefer to write up a scope of work or throw together some interview slides. But that's like building a house without a set of drawings—you and your team are making it up as you go along. And none of you are on the same page. Working to uncover the message through an iterative process of trial and error will result in the highest probability of persuading the client to select you.

Bring the client into development of your strategy

You must guard again becoming isolated during the process of strategizing. The competitive process is not a game of Charades in which you're not allowed to speak. By all means, share your thought process with your client. There's no better way to develop trust than to include them in your team's brainstorming during early development of your strategy.

A meeting with the client is an opportunity to exchange ideas, while gauging their reaction. If you aren't the incumbent, then your pitch must be compelling and significantly different from the pitch offered by your competition if you want to stand out. If the client reacts favorably, then you're on the right track! Return to the office and keep building and strengthening your strategy by fleshing out details.

If the client responds unfavorably to your strategy, then go back to the drawing board and re-formulate your

> *A war-story on what not to do: An RFP arrived which staff felt sure they could win. Enthusiasm grew, and technical staff was convinced they were "the best." One admitted weakness was lack of recent client contact. We sent three people to the pre-proposal meeting. A site tour confirmed that our ideas, approach, and innovations would win hands-down. A few weeks after the proposal was submitted, we were notified that we were not shortlisted.*
>
> *There was great dismay among our people, and talk of how the selection process must have been rigged. Firms invited to interview had been doing repeat work for this client. We were convinced in our own minds that our experience and technology were better. However, we lacked competitive knowledge – no one had done their homework on the qualifications of the winning firm. They just assumed we were superior. Moreover, lack of client contact doomed us.*
>
> *If you are not an incumbent, then you must formulate a compelling competitive strategy. Resting strategy on the laurels of "we're the best" is repeatedly the path to landslide defeat.*
>
> *Meeting with the client, starting one year prior to the RFP, to understand their needs and test our ideas for their project could have resulted in a successful outcome, we are convinced.*

ideas, using the client's feedback. Obviously, this iterative approach takes time and it can't be accomplished very well once the procurement documents have been released. This reinforces the need to start early – sometimes a year or more in advance.

Some people worry that ideas presented to the client could be leaked to the competition. This is indeed a concern, but in our experience this risk is less than that posed by never receiving feedback or an unfavorable reaction. Also, most "secret weapons" never work. Many are gimmicky and can be easily undone. A secret weapon could be a "big name" teaming partner, or a renowned expert in their field, for example. Instead, focus on the fundamental competitive strategy – if you think you need a secret weapon to win, you're probably reaching for straws and should no-go the pursuit.

Instead of being overly concerned with your best ideas being shared, strive for continuous improvement in your competitive strategy. By assuming that your ideas do become known, go the extra mile to enhance your messages and proofs.

Communicating Competitive Strategies

After you've been around the block a few times with your pursuit team, and your differentiating strategies begin to crystallize, it is time to get the messages right. A well-conceived competitive strategy is useless if it is not articulated in a form that is easy to understand and memorable. As illustrated in the example at the beginning of this chapter, the grammatical construction of "feature-*verb*-**benefit**," followed by appropriate proofs, is a great starting point, such as:

- The Jones Consulting team's design concept *saves* **millions in construction costs**
- Smith Group's creative design *will deliver* **a world-class showcase facility**
- Combining technical innovation and stakeholder outreach *wins* **community acceptance**
- New control system software *enhances* **operator safety**

Supporting points must then be developed to enhance the basic competitive strategy. Great claims are worth nothing if they are not proven. Rarely does a firm win by making only one point. Then, messages and proofs need to be interwoven. Let's expand on the first example:

<u>The Jones Consulting team's design concept</u> *saves* **millions in construction costs and shortens the schedule by six months.**
- Rebuilding the facilities, instead of replacing them, results in $3 million in reduced construction costs
- Our team completed a similar rehabilitation project in a nearby town, which resulted in cost savings to that client
- The concept's shorter schedule eases permit requirements, reducing the reliance on regulators to meet their deadlines
- Bill Jones will serve as Project Manager and devote 80% of his available time to keep the project on-track
- Our design staff understands your standards and procedures, based on previous projects we have performed for you, reducing review time

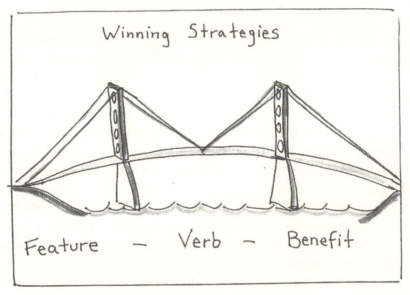

We identify an important overall, interlinked, competitive strategy (saving money and time), explain how we would achieve it (rebuilding), prove it (project completed nearby), offer up the firm's leader as the Project Manager (delivering a "star" manager is always a solid competitive strategy), identified ease of permitting (as another benefit linked to the shorter schedule), and reduce the time needed for client review of documents (we know their standards).

As we said earlier, sometimes saving money is not the most attractive differentiator. A competitor to Jones Consulting (Smith Group, who is trying to break-in to this client) might propose an alternative approach that appeals to a different emotion:

<u>Smith Group's creative design</u> *will deliver* **a world-class showcase facility.**
- The project team has worked around the clock to innovate the original design concept
- Superior facilities will provide a "legacy" for your Board of Directors, attract more customers, and increase return on your investment
- We have a successful track record on four recent projects, all of which were under budget
- Smith Group has studied your standards and procedures in detail (which neutralizes Jones Consulting's contention that their past work with the client gives them an advantage)

Smith Group identifies a *different* competitive strategy (a better facility, one that will be forever linked to the members of the Board), tells how they worked hard (staying up late developing design concepts, so the client may question how hard the incumbent has worked), shows why their idea is better (more customers mean more money), proves it (four recent, successful, projects), and added value (Smith hasn't worked for this client before, but compensated by going the extra mile to study their standards and procedures).

Could this win? Of course it could. Note some aspects of this competitive strategy:
- Smith's concept appeals to a "hot button" they uncovered from their discussions with the decision-makers (providing a legacy project). They additionally explain that a facility which achieves acclaim could attract more customers, increasing revenues. **Many sales pitches stop short with a tall boast, taking for granted that the client shares enthusiasm for the benefit.**
- Smith differentiates itself with their approach. They know that Jones has a track record with the client. Smith presents an innovative idea of making money as opposed to saving money.
- Smith makes a memorable pitch, using "world-class" and "showcase" as sound bites. While this will not appeal to everyone (especially the frugal), they tested this with the client informally, in discussions prior to release of the RFP, and received favorable feedback.

- Smith also sends an important message: that they are "hungry" to earn the client's work. They worked around the clock, investing more time than the Jones team. This has a chance of "wowing" the client with a superior effort. They back it up by overcoming the weakness of not having worked for the client before, by learning their standards (on their own dime, but very visibly to the client). Perhaps they will even be able to offer improvements to the client's procedures.

Who will win? It's hard to say, and likely this will be a close call, and could boil down to a comparison of values among the strongest personalities on the selection committee. Both competitive strategies are equally compelling.

It is important to note that these firms would have worked on their competitive strategies over a long period of time. Each held regular internal marketing meetings in which the action plan was advanced. As questions arose, key individuals we assigned to uncover information, test ideas, and spend time with the client to learn more about their likes and dislikes. At each successive meeting, the competitive strategies were refined, and every word used to deliver the strategy was examined until the pursuit teams were united in their support of the approach. This is the type of effort it takes on many competitive pursuits.

Additional Pointers on Competitive Strategies

After a competition, particularly a close one, always debrief with your client—win or lose. Listen carefully (without leading the witness) to their recollections of your proposal and messages, and how your strategy compared with the competition. Look for the client to repeat some of your own messages or sound bites – for successful pursuits these will resonate with the client for quite some time.

You may be surprised by what the client remembers from the pursuit, especially if you won. Even with all your positioning, clients make decisions for their own reasons. You should verify that their reasons match what you intended to communicate.

Major pursuits are expensive in not only time and money, but emotional energy. Be sure to learn from your experiences; sometimes this is the only return on investment you may receive from placing second.

While this may seem obvious, what does it mean if you cannot come up with a competitive strategy? Try as you might, every attempt to overcome an inherent weakness in your team, or a competitor's strengths, leaves you flat. Then it's probably time for you to make a no-go decision. The earlier you learn this, the better. And the earlier in the pursuit you are able to do so, the more money and energy you will save to invest in another opportunity where your chances of winning are greater.

Does it ever make sense to pull the plug on an ongoing pursuit, even as it transitions from positioning to RFP, and onto proposal preparation? Of course it does; don't throw good money after bad. If a reality check tells you that it's just not winnable after tracking it for some time, then be brave, and make a no-go decision.

The boss says, "This upcoming design project is a must-win. I've thought about all the ways we could approach this. I've decided we're going to use my favorite competitive strategy: overwhelming force."

You groan because you know what this means; it calls for leaving no stone un-

> *War Story:* Two project pursuits for the same client, set apart by six months. On the first, the competitive strategy is to provide a fully developed solution. The project team goes to the interview ready to "hit the ground running." We are not selected.
>
> A competitor had brought in flow charts, workshop ideas, and decision-making approaches. They stressed processes for reaching the right answer. They brought no solutions. The client says, "you impressed us with your solution, but it seemed your mind was made up. We didn't think we could influence your plans."
>
> Six months later; same client, new RFP. Instead of pre-engineering the project, our competitive strategy is to present tools and methods for collaborative decision-making. A week later, the client notifies us that we've lost, again. A competitor had come in with the project fully analyzed, and 2-3 workable solutions. The client says, "even though you impressed us with your ability to facilitate decisions, the winning firm was ready to go."
>
> Infuriating? Clients can change their mind, especially over time. For both proposals, our weakness was in not reality-checking our competitive strategy. All competitive strategies require recent validation with the buyer.
>
> Many technical professionals reel at this story, throwing up their arms in surrender. They see it as proof of their frustration with business development. Sometimes it's hard to argue. The best marketers are left grinning.

turned, and practically throwing the entire company at the pursuit.

You had already written off the pursuit as unwinnable, but you agree to take a fresh look. You spend as much time with the client as possible, working to understand the selection committee's "hot buttons."

You convene a pursuit team of company experts. You groom the competitive advantages of "cheaper, better, and faster." You find your best project manager in the company. He signs an agreement to relocate. You approach people who know the incumbent firm working for the client. The competitor's preliminary report is scrutinized, and the team identifies over $10 million in savings. You vet the ideas with the client, who is enthusiastic about your fresh look at his project.

You evaluate local teaming partners, incorporating their ideas and allowing them to objectively assess your strategies. Your proposed project manager goes all-out and works with company experts to pre-engineer three different alternative project solutions. These are previewed to the client.

Your marketing staff focuses their effort on preparing a knock-out proposal and interview presentation. The reasons to select your firm are clearly understood by everyone who reviews the documents.

Needless to say, you win the project and get the promotion you had been hoping for.

Chapter 4
Positioning to Improve your Chance of Winning

> *"Luck is what happens when preparation meets opportunity."*
> *- Seneca, 5BC – 65AD*

    I had never witnessed such challenging effort as our positioning for a major assignment with one of the largest cities in the United States. The City's wastewater utility had failed to meet key provisions of the Clean Water Act and they needed technical assistance. At stake for our firm was not only a new contract, but a strategic opportunity to leverage the assignment into similar services for other agencies. However, we had a big hill to climb; our competition had worked hard to create this particular project. With more experience under their belt, they were able to meet with the client to plant the seeds, then later develop a detailed, shared understanding of the scope of work.

    Leadership of our pursuit was taken up by one of the firm's masters, a marketing genius whose brilliance was surpassed only by his hard work and passion for winning. He brought in senior people from around the country, as well as rising stars who would benefit from the learning experience. At times, the pursuit team grew to 25 individuals, sequestered in a conference room, working on the proposal and the interview. There was much ground to be gained, and it was quite an experience watching the pursuit leader direct the team. But what I wanted to know was, "How were they going to win the job?"

    From our perspective, positioning is a term that encompasses the act of improving your chances of selection for a competitive opportunity. Ideally, the goal of positioning is to become established as the front-runner. Capture plans (also known as pursuit plans or campaign strategies) are the written documentation of positioning activities, competitive strategy, and other plans for closing the sale.

A marketing approach that is based on waiting for RFPs to arrive is a reactive and self-defeating exercise. On the other hand, a proactive approach of planning and positioning for the projects on which you want to work will empower your firm to control its destiny. Of the major changes in the technical services industry in the last 20 years, the shift to early identification and active positioning is one of the most significant. We are constantly preaching the importance of positioning for achieving sales goals. We have to; our competitors are doing the same.

Any company can respond to an unanticipated RFP. In fact, clients hope you will because they need to create competition. So, they distribute RFPs to a variety of firms, hoping that at least several will submit proposals. But here's the catch: most of the time, clients have already established a front-runner before the RFPs are even issued. And it's someone who has already shown interest in the project.

> We recall, when we were starting out, talking to the lead "marketing guy." We were anxious to learn. His chore was to evaluate new RFPs and determine which ones the firm would pursue. But he told us that his biggest problem was that our engineers tried to pursue them all. Every RFP was viewed with the same outlook: "We can do the work - we're the best." We asked why this was such a problem, and why we couldn't just submit proposals on all of them?
>
> He then gave us advice which we will never forget. "Listen," he said. "Engineers think they can win everything because they're smart. But competition is fierce, and it takes more to win than just being smart.
>
> "We must get to know the clients, and they need to get to know us. We also need to do our homework by developing technical solutions, and propose ideas for resolving issues, such as public acceptance and environmental compliance. All this means work to develop a proposal then, if shortlisted, more work preparing for an interview."
>
> Doing good work is necessary, but not sufficient, to winning. A lot of other things have to be done, and there are not enough hours in the day to pour the necessary effort into every RFP.

You may convince yourself that no other firm has anticipated an RFP, but make no mistake, someone always has. Firms who submit proposals without prior knowledge of the RFP, and for which no positioning was accomplished, are spending their precious business development dollars solely to support another firm's well-positioned selection for the prize.

Why is positioning for a competition so difficult?

- First, technical professionals often do not see the value of positioning, because they receive little or no marketing or sales training in college. They have to learn "on the job." Some learn to tolerate it, but many do not fully engage in a productive way.
- Second, sales and marketing require human contact and interaction. Very few sales are made without advance client contact, and so the introverted nature of many technical professionals limits their effectiveness in positioning activities.

Again, we see the dynamic tension between rocket science and art. Overcoming these obstacles becomes the key to a healthy, sustainable success rate in competing for and winning new work. This new work is necessary for a firm (and therefore you) to stay in business.

Successful sales programs use methods that take advantage of the inherent strengths of technical staff by breaking down positioning into logical steps of analysis and action, which should be managed as one might approach a technical project. A major purpose of marketers is to organize, facilitate, and keep positioning on track.

Positioning for a sale is accomplished through a number of activities, including:

- Client Contact
- Technical Development and Understanding
- Visibility
- Teaming
- Politics
- Procurement

Client Contact

While other aspects of the process bring value, **client contact is the single most important form of positioning for new work**. Nothing else is even close. Why is this so? One of the best perspectives we've seen on this came from a former CEO: "The assets of a technical professional services firm walk out the door every day at closing time." While technology is vitally important, this is a service industry, and the service is performed by people for other people, face-to-face. Therefore, we believe nothing is more compelling, valuable, or productive than a meeting between seller and buyer. Yet face-to-face client contact is challenging for many technical professionals. Hence they resort to other forms of positioning, such as visibility, advertising, and blind submittals, all to avoid sitting in front of a client. These other activities are worthwhile, but there is no substitute for meetings in which one can pose questions, receive informative responses, and read the nuances of body language. Non-verbal feedback inherent in a face-to-face meeting is invaluable, and irreplaceable.

We often witness heated discussions on what constitutes a face-to-face client contact. Quality interaction is paramount, so ideally the meeting should be face-to-face in the client's office. Phone calls are useful, but not as valuable. By comparison, a polite wave across the room during a crowded technical conference does not count as a client contact; little interaction with clients on meaningful issues takes place at these functions.

What to Accomplish at a Positioning Meeting

Obtaining an appointment with a buyer is invaluable, so the time should be treated as a precious commodity. The nature and content of a conversation during a client contact should be actively planned and carefully executed.

> *Harold credits a mentor for what he calls* ***"The rule of seven."*** *Over the years, the mentor responded to repeated inquiries of how many client contacts were required to be considered "positioned" for a project. He grew frustrated with the inane focus on exactitude. Finally, he threw up his hands and pronounced that seven was the minimum number of contacts. Strangely, this answer was accepted with little protest from the technical professionals. No further proofs, theorems, charts, graphs, or differential equations were required.*
>
> *So, we have found that seven is a sufficiently high enough number to prevent most technical professionals from ever attaining it, and is therefore a good goal.*
>
> *Keep in mind that no number of meetings will ensure formation of a solid relationship. In fact, there is a chance that by the seventh meeting, the opposite could result— one or both of you could dislike each other. We talk more about relationship-building in this book, but there are no guarantees that time always results in good relationships.*

- <u>Introduction</u>. If you have never met the client before, then this is a classic "cold call." Introduce yourself, be brief, and then let the client take the lead. Your first meeting is definitely not the time for a long recant of your curriculum vitae. The old saying that there is only one chance to make a first impression is true, so treat carefully the first five minutes of any client meeting.

- <u>Listen and learn</u>. Another great marketer and mentor once said that "marketing is information." The client contact meeting is the place to gather the information which forms an understanding of a client's needs, including the background and purpose of the assignment you are seeking. "Drivers" are important to understand, as they constitute the reason behind the need. In addition, it is important to understand the client's "hot buttons." These are the issues which cause the client to sit on the edge of their seat. (A good way to draw these out is to ask what keeps them "up at night"). You're trying to understand their hopes and fears. Understand that many technical professionals and marketers think that this information can be gleaned from the RFP when it arrives at the office! It won't be there.

- <u>Engage in technical discussions</u>. To the dismay of most technical professionals, not every client wants to drill down into the gory details of engineering and science. However, patience will be rewarded by an engaging discussion of technical issues. If there is one part of client contact meetings that even introverts can enjoy, this is it. If you are predominantly a marketer, you may reach your "knowledge ceiling." But that's okay. In our experience, seasoned clients respect the fact that no individual can be an expert at everything. In fact, the technical questions of a meeting most often result in opportunities for additional visits with subject matter experts.

- <u>Building or strengthening a relationship</u>. Over time, by getting to know one another, a relationship may develop between the client and the professional services provider. The value of information will improve in proportion to the number of meetings, as the strength of the relationship grows. If you're a client reading this, such meetings should be "double-entry" transactions. You receive as much as you give. The buyer gains from the knowledge imparted by a seller; the seller gains in knowledge of the buyer.

- <u>Planting seeds, testing ideas, and observing reactions</u>. At some point in the positioning process, you offer ideas. The act of sharing thoughts and gaining feedback helps the technical professional make incremental improvements in their winning strategy. This proactive testing of ideas helps to discard concepts which are not well received and supports acceptance of good ideas when the client reads the proposal.

- <u>Educating and/or informing the client</u>. Sometimes a client contact meeting is arranged with the express purpose of presenting new information. The intended purpose of the meeting is often "educational," but the wise marketer will not make this the "stated reason," unless arrogance is the message to be left in the client's mind. When they are sincerely interested in learning, clients welcome technical professionals. Legions of deli owners have made fortunes by catering brown-bag luncheons sponsored by companies hoping to parlay the sharing of information into new business. We like the brown-bag approach, and truthfully find it to be underused. Be realistic in expectations. Present no more than two or three ideas. Information overload leads to saturation, and can be a turn-off. Conversations and interactive dialogue are more important than whatever new technology you are featuring. These events can serve to build a working relationship before an RFP is received.

- <u>Wrestling with difficult or challenging issues</u>. For almost all major opportunities, there will be challenging issues. One of the best examples of this is the client's budget falling short of the technical professional's estimate. How many times have we seen the client dismiss a proposal, even though it was clearly the best, because they simply could not afford the approach? If the client can't afford your "ballpark" price, then it's better to know early, so there is time for the rocket scientists to go back to drawing board and develop an alternative approach. If it can't be found, then declare failure early, call an end to the pursuit, and save your time and money for a better day and a new opportunity. Many other issues are complex, controversial, or political. Why are they so often avoided until the moment of truth at an interview? Tough topics are clearly better covered with the client well in advance of the formal procurement. By carefully raising these points early with clients, you'll save both parties a lot of heartache.

If the technical professional or marketer is an active listener during a client meeting, then feedback may be detected via non-verbal signs. The most important non-verbal signal is the sign that the meeting is over. When the client glances at their watch, clears their throat, or pushes away from the conference room table, you have less than 30 seconds to wrap up the meeting.

Naturally, incumbents have an advantage in conducting client contacts. They have already established relationships, and meetings naturally occur during the course of their everyday business with their client. Most clients already have technical professionals working for them; therefore they often aren't interested in developing another relationship with a similar service provider (do YOU really want two telephone services at the same time?). But many clients realize their current firm can't do everything.

It can be hard for the technical professional to form an effective relationship in early meetings with a prospective client. Since you aren't actually working for them, you are highly unlikely to build trust that can be earned or proven. Coming in from the cold on a large opportunity will have unique challenges. As a result, sometimes positioning for a major pursuit requires first capturing a smaller project, so the client can "test drive" your firm.

The 80-20 Rule of Client Meetings

Two of the greatest foibles of client contact meetings are thinking that you 1) need to know everything, and 2) talking constantly to show your knowledge. These could not be further from the desired goal of a face-to-face meeting. The importance of active listening is well documented in other books, but wise marketers know that no one ever learned anything while talking. Such meetings should follow the 80-20 rule, where the client talks 80% of the time, while the technical professional or marketer listens.

> *The person asking the questions is in control of the meeting because he/she is steering the conversation. The more your 20% of the discussion is in the form of questions, the more you will learn from the 80% of your listening, because the client is talking about what you want to know.*

Of course, the seller needs to ask some questions, and clarifying responses are important. In addition, if the client consented to the meeting as a means of genuinely getting to know you, your company, or something about a great idea you may have, then you'll be expected to talk. Stick to the 80-20 rule, present an idea, then shut-up! Listen for the response, and you'll learn a great deal.

We are often asked if it is appropriate to take notes during client contacts. Note-taking signifies that you value the information you're receiving. If we were a client rattling off important numbers, and you didn't take notes, we'd either think you had a photographic memory (unlikely), didn't care, or weren't smart enough to take advantage of the free information.

However, taking copious notes is not advisable. The client could get the feeling that they're a witness at a deposition. You should take some brief notes, but not so many that writing overtakes active listening. We suggest jotting down key words; then, after the meeting is over, you can expand on your notes. Some marketers do this right afterward, in the client's parking lot. Later, at the office, prepare a client contact report while everything is fresh in your mind. Sometimes it can be effective to bring a more junior member of your staff to take notes.

> *We once observed a junior staff member make a mistake while working on an assignment at a client's office. This was a new client, with the prospect of growing a small project into a multi-million dollar engagement. Instructions to the staff member were sent via email. He was directed to be doubly aggressive in his service to the client because the company "was hoping to secure a greater amount of work."*
>
> *Unfortunately, the junior person printed the email and took it with him to the meeting. With the shuffle of papers, a hardcopy of the email was left behind; the client found it and did not take well to being the target of our plotting of next steps to secure a big prize.*
>
> *Management had to do a lot of tap-dancing to keep from being fired, and the junior person was taken off the assignment.* <u>*Take care of your notes, client reports, and email the way Colonel Sanders cares for his fried chicken recipe!*</u>

This approach serves a secondary purpose of introducing more people from the firm, and offers field training at the same time.

Many senior staff do not prepare written client contact notes for reasons which never ceases to amaze us. Most frequently heard are that there isn't enough time, they forgot, or "Who else needs to know, I have it taken care of." To this, we say, "baloney." It's a critical part of teamwork. **Nearly every project of the size that can keep a team busy must be won by a team.**

Marketing is a costly investment. Factoring in travel costs for mileage, air fare, meals, and lodging, one can see the cost of a single client meeting reaching into the hundreds, if not thousands of dollars. Even the briefest of client contact reports become the central vehicle for communicating findings to other team members. As has been said previously, marketing is information; sharing that information improves the value of the investment to your company.

A rule of thumb might be that the client contact report should take less than half the time to write than the appointment itself. We've observed some technical professionals preparing dissertations, with multiple drafts, wearing out word processing staff. Don't do this; the purpose is to efficiently communicate the most important facts of the meeting.

Distribute client contact reports only to those who need to know. They rarely should be printed. Aside from the obvious sustainability benefits, printed client contact reports can find their way into the wrong hands (see sidebar). We're constantly amazed at seeing these reports sitting at the laser printer for days. Your future livelihoods depend on that proprietary information.

If your meetings raise sensitive information, don't put it in writing. Getting to know a particular client's preferences and attitudes is an important goal for client contacts. However, if that information is put in writing, and gets back to the client, you may lose the procurement. Most importantly for client contact reports, be sure to recommend action items, assignments, and the timing of the next contact. Your marketing staff can use these recommendations to schedule additional positioning activities.

Scheduling and Following Through on Client Contacts

We find it easy during positioning meetings to develop long lists of clients to visit. Follow-through is another matter. While some technical professionals are better at this than others, the plain fact is that most procrastinate when it comes to scheduling client meetings, especially with individuals whom they do not know very well. Cold calls inevitably fall to the bottom of the priority list, somewhere near "getting more exercise," "learning a second language," and other New Year's resolutions.

Fortunately, there are some methods to ensure that these appointments are made and kept. This is where a marketing coordinator can have a big impact by doing a few small but important things. First, the marketing coordinator should take the lead in creating and maintaining a calendar of scheduled client contacts. Identifying the precise date for each appointment is not required; it is good enough to note the proposed meetings each month, or even quarter. Then, the marketing coordinator could set up the client appointments. This doesn't work for all clients, but helps set a tone regarding the importance of client positioning. Pairing introverted technical professionals with extroverted individuals can be another technique for getting people out the door, away from their desks, to see clients. Breaking the ice on a cold call with two people offers safety in numbers.

We're often asked if a marketing coordinator should meet directly with clients, with or without the technical professional. The answer is, "that depends." If a staff member, technical or otherwise, can develop effective relationships, they should be encouraged. The downside is that marketing coordinators may not understand the technical subject matter of the firm. This isn't always a negative, however. Marketers are less likely to be buried in technical minutiae, and focus more on the relationship. Marketing coordinators can be especially effective at social gatherings, such as luncheons, conference receptions, and other events. Many firms overlook marketing coordinators as assets in these roles, and we think that's a mistake.

> Not every client contact should be a sales event. If you're always seen as pursuing a sale, then you'll always be regarded as a salesperson. A great marketing mentor said, "the best time to sell is when the client isn't buying." Clients are bombarded by firms making sales calls. It's not long before they become so saturated that every firm looks the same.
>
> Consider the long view. Imagine a pursuit that is a year away from an RFP. During that year, the magic 7 client contacts could take place at different venues. Alternating locations brings different insights. Interacting with clients at professional conferences, at public meetings, or in social settings is of immense value. If the client is not on guard, they will be more relaxed.
>
> Observing people, their behavior, and their attitudes under different conditions away from their day-to-day routine can offer tremendous insights. You can learn a lot from clients when you aren't selling.

Technical Development/ Project Understanding

There is widespread belief that technical development is a proposal activity, to be initiated upon receipt of the RFP. On the contrary, depending on complexity, it can be an active component of positioning. Gaining clarity and formulating technical solutions are important positioning activities. Prior to issuance of the RFP, firms have "Golden Time" where they can test their ideas with the client. This is an opportunity to prove that you know the project and its challenges. You can invest the time to identify insights that go beyond the client's knowledge, proving that hiring your firm adds value.

Your team should evaluate and prepare a technical approach to solving the project's challenges. This may require substantial effort and expense. Defense contractors are good examples where marketing and proposal costs can easily reach millions of dollars, because they are required to pre-engineer systems. In some cases, for professional engineering firms engaged in alternative project delivery methods, the design must be completed to a point where a construction contractor can prepare a cost estimate, indeed a Guaranteed Maximum Price (GMP). Your team will have to exercise judgment in allocating marketing dollars to invest in the pre-engineering for a very large positioning effort.

> *If you're a client, do you know who pays the cost of proposal efforts? We all do. Firms can spend millions of dollars on technical professional pursuits. Competition drives technical professionals to do more in order to win. Sellers and buyers have created an upward spiral of marketing efforts and costs.*
>
> *We recognize the importance of competition and the need for clients to conduct a transparent, fair selection process. Recognition of the cost of competition benefits all of us, because it creates an awareness to keep the process efficient, open, and fair.*

Internal meetings structured as workshops are a good approach for developing ideas. Technical professionals are usually willing to donate their time and ideas, in return for a box lunch. If possible, conduct joint meetings with the client to increase the interaction and immediately gauge their reaction to ideas.

Activities for technical development and project understanding include:

- Brainstorming technical ideas and concepts; formulating alternative solutions.

- Developing a method of approach, including a scope of work. A flowchart of tasks and activities is helpful, especially if time-scaled.
- Initiating field investigations (site visit and photos, don't forget shots of key staff on-site for use in the proposal and interview).
- Researching old reports, data, technical memos, or news clippings.
- Interviewing project stakeholders from the client's organization, as well as outsiders (e.g., customers, special interest groups, impacted public, regulators, and elected officials).
- Preparing supporting graphics (flow charts, maps, schematics, designs).
- Estimating preliminary costs (construction costs and professional services).
- Conducting value engineering workshops.
- Developing prototypes (e.g., software, pilot plants, and experimental bench-scale tests).
- Touring previous projects with the client. There's nothing like a site visit to past successful work. If your tour or demo can include a testimonial, this is a decided plus.

Be sure to evaluate work done for the client by other firms, especially if the incumbent is a competitor. Keep in mind that the client may have a vested interest in previous work because they paid for it. A tempting competitive strategy of "goring the ox" (work by previous firms) may make the client look bad at the same time.

Some clients may honestly be interested in a fresh look. When called upon to critique the work of others, your professional bedside manner could set the tone for moving the client away from an idea fostered by the incumbent. Look for ways to improve ideas by others, not criticize them. In our chapter on Competitive Strategies, we discuss the hunt for ways of being cheaper, better, and faster. Many of the ideas which form the basis of winning strategies are founded in the technical development stage and based on a solid understanding of the project.

Teaming

Forming a project team is another important part of positioning. In fact, a project team constituted solely by members of your own firm is a rarity nowadays. There are a number of valid reasons to team, including:

- Skills. This is the number one reason for teaming with another firm – because your own company may not have all of the exper-

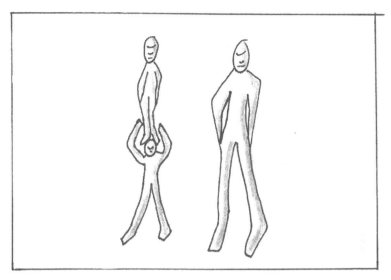

  tise needed to perform the work. With increasing complexity of projects and assignments, you are likely to partner with specialists who meet unique needs.
- Experience. In some cases, your firm may also lack experience in the subject technology or method of approach. Teaming with another firm that has more experience could potentially make the client more comfortable, especially if your company boasts strength of relationships, and a teaming partner increases your qualifications.
- Capacity. If the project is large, you may not have enough resources to complete the work on time. As with other sales points, put yourself in the client's shoes in evaluating whether your firm can perform the work, or if help is needed. Anytime teaming among firms occurs, a certain amount of efficiency is lost. So, the team will need to persuade the client that an amalgam of firms is as efficient as a single large firm.
- Location. If the client or project resides in a geography where you do not have staff, establishing a local presence can be critical. Partnering with a local firm will bring a better understanding of local conditions. Responsive service is an added benefit, if the project team is within easy driving distance of the client.

- **Preference**. The client may express a preference for certain firms or skilled individuals. Bringing them onto the team is the best form of obtaining the votes of a selection committee.
- **Requirement**. Many clients establish procurement set-asides for specific categories of firms – commonly for small and/or disadvantaged businesses (e.g., woman, minority, veteran, disabled veteran, native American-owned). This is increasingly prevalent for the Federal government, as well as large clients with interest in outreach to firms whose ownership is reflective of their constituents.
- **Risk**. A firm may elect to pool the risk of a project, by spreading it out over more than one firm. If selected, then the project risk can potentially be better absorbed with more than one partner conducting the work. Sharing proposal development costs also can be accomplished by teaming.
- **Reducing Competition**. This one is sometimes not well received by clients. It is possible to narrow the field and eliminate a competitor by joining forces through teaming. Or, "if you can't beat them, join them." Considering the individual strengths and weaknesses of any given firm, competitive odds are improved by firms that have teamed with a strong partner to whom they may have otherwise lost. Obviously, there will be a smaller piece of the pie to each member of the successful team. On the other hand, members of the losing teams walk away empty-handed.

We have experienced a tendency for technical professionals to defer teaming until final procurement documents are released. Presumably, waiting affords them the opportunity to see all of the final conditions of the RFP, prior to making a commitment. We often think that people who subscribe to this type of rationale probably also wait until age 50 to marry and start a family, just to ensure they have found the perfect spouse. In reality, almost all of the pertinent information needed to justify teaming is known quite early in most pursuits. Moreover, if you wait too long, all of the good dance partners may already be taken.

Always, always check out potential teaming partners with the client. You can have all of the internal debates that you want, but ultimately the client is the final judge of your teaming efforts.

We commonly are asked whether you should talk to more than one potential teaming partner at a time. There is a lot to be gained by networking, including learning more about other firms, so we're in favor of these types of conversations. Getting to know your competition is of long-term benefit, regardless of whether you get married on the first date. However, be forewarned. There are firms that "go fishing," being more interested in scoping you out than in actually teaming. In order to be effective, teams must evolve to full disclosure with one another, as if the other team's employees were their own. Getting to know teaming partners and developing a high level of trust over time will help avoid shallow inquiries of no real, immediate benefit.

We are also frequently asked whether to be an exclusive partner to a single team, especially when you will not be the prime contractor. We believe that being exclusive brings focus and avoids the temptation to share strategies or secrets with another partner. Alternatively, if you are a subconsultant whose service is a commodity, it makes business sense to climb aboard more than one team to increase your odds of winning.

Teaming Agreements

Recognize that teaming can take time. Teaming inquiries are typically met with the need to validate the other firm's strengths, as described above. We think teaming agreements are essential. Robert Frost wrote, "good fences make good neighbors." Establishing in writing the promises, expectations, and boundaries of teaming partners avoids costly and emotional misunderstandings once the work is under contract. Reviewing a written teaming agreement also sprinkles the participants with a healthy dose of reality. Handshake agreements can be forgotten as staffing changes or acquisitions occur. We have been part of long-term teams in which firms were acquired during the course of the pursuit; an agreement for future pursuits kept the team together.

We have used simple teaming agreements as short as a single page. If your attorneys get involved, teaming agreements begin to look more like a contract. It is important to get some teaming conditions, especially monetary quotations, in writing, where price is a deciding factor. This tends to be more important where commodities or supplies are incorporated into the technical professional's contract. In some cases, these prices can run into the millions of dollars, so firm written quotations are a necessity. Obviously, written specifications and, for engineers, drawings or plans, serve as the basis for price quotations which then become bound into the subcontract agreement.

All teaming agreements should have an expiration date. If the procurement becomes delayed, market conditions can change. Other firms can position, and you may find your partner's strengths can be weakened through the efforts of the competition. Protect against this is by contractually "sunsetting" the teaming agreement, triggering a re-evaluation by both parties. In our experience, six months to a year is appropriate timing. Obviously, a teaming agreement should also expire if the client materially changes the scope of the procurement, or if you're not selected.

Finally, all technical firms must recognize that it is the client who calls the shots. If anything about the winning team is unacceptable to the client, then the team must acknowledge this, and take appropriate action. We have seen situations where one of the teaming partners has been forced to step down from the team, trade places between prime and sub, or even change key personnel in response to the client's wishes.

Ethical Political Strategies

This book could not possibly do justice to the topic of politics, as it relates to business development. But some brief insights may be helpful, especially as there is little written on the topic. No discussion of politics should be held at a professional services firm (or any other, for that matter) without a companion discussion of ethical behavior. The two go hand-in-hand.

The word "politics" refers to the role of elected (and typically non-technical) or appointed officials in selection processes. As described earlier, selection committee decisions are frequently ratified or approved by elected or appointed officials. In some instances, a representative from the governing body may participate in the selection committee. For some clients, these governing bodies may make the selection decisions entirely themselves.

For larger opportunities, the stakes are raised, and with them the livelihoods of a lot of people, on both sides of the procurement. Under these circumstances, a great deal of discussion must be focused on influencing politicians for the successful outcome of a selection process. In some rare cases, politics may be all that matters – a rude awakening for many technical professionals.

It may be difficult to detect politics coming into play at first. Some indicators include:

- Announcement of decisions by selection committees take longer than they should.
- The client has a track record of changing its mind once initial decisions are reached.
- You receive reports from staff that a "higher authority" is engaged.
- Firms who benefit from procurement requirements have unusually close relationships with politicians and/or select high-level staff, rather than with the technical staff directly involved in the project.
- You find yourself or others in your firm receiving invitations to contribute to political campaigns.

It is important to keep in mind that politics are not always a factor in a decision-making process, even if one or more of the indicators are present. On the other hand, if you believe that politics are involved in a selection process, we counsel great caution.

Historically, internal discussions of politics have been off-limits to all but a few people in the corner offices. However, as a marketer, you must be pragmatic, and never lose sight of the fact that all decisions are, in the end, value judgments. As such, there is rarely a right or wrong position, answer, or opinion. We have found that staying neutral and avoiding announced political stands has served us well. It is important to keep in mind that elected officials have a role to play and it will be to your benefit to engage and understand. They are decision-makers to be influenced by you, but within strict bounds of conduct.

You may need to engage with lobbyists who have forged relationships with elected officials and are experts in understanding local political processes. Although the lobbying industry is viewed by many with a jaundiced eye, we don't see it that way. Lobbyists provide a valuable service, like you, to develop greater understanding in the minds of decision-makers through education on complex topics or issues. How else would an ordinary member of a community, elected to an office, learn the intricacies of a 1,000 page Federal farm subsidy bill? By reading it? Or by listening to informed people providing their insight?

Be forewarned that there are laws for engaging lobbyists, for their conduct, and that they can be costly. The most successful relationships with lobbyists incorporate specific goals, with a plan and a schedule for achieving desired results.

A word of caution on the role of campaign contributions. In your interaction with elected officials, it is highly likely that you will be asked for assistance in financing their campaigns. We find there is a lot of misunderstanding about how the process works, especially when it comes to expectations in return for contributions made. This can be a very slippery slope for the beginner, which can not only be expensive, but a lot can go wrong if you aren't careful in following the rules.

Do nothing unless you know the rules or laws for what you are doing, and are certain that you are within legal, ethical, and moral bounds. Rules for campaign contributions are often posted online, and you should be aware that there can be major differences from one agency to another in allowable amounts, frequency, source, and other details. Be sure to study and understand the rules, and if you are unclear, then do not participate until you can secure expert advice. There can be severe direct and indirect consequences for bad choices. While some level of financial political support can be legal, any connection made between a contribution and a favorable decision may cause you to be talking to your children through a small hole in a Plexiglas window.

The most important point to be made is that decisions on procurements are complex. Never underestimate the number of people who will be involved in selecting which firm receives the work. Your job is to "know" as much as possible about the process, to position as well as possible, and proceed with a clear understanding of the playing field.

Pursuing Projects when not Positioned

When do you submit a proposal "to get our name in there?" A strategy to submit a proposal simply to increase your visibility to a targeted client is age-old. Presumably, the desired impact is to further your firm's positioning for future opportunities by being "noticed" favorably as the result of your proposal. The dilemma is that preparing a proposal is expensive, period. Though we have heard some technical professionals remark that "it's no big deal" because most of the work falls onto the marketing coordinators, we find that reasoning to be invalid. If you believe a marketer is going to pull off a good proposal without significant contribution from technical staff, then you're not much of a team player. Preparing one that gets you "noticed" is time consuming. In addition, if shortlisted, you will not be able to decline attending an interview, adding to the cost and effort.

To all of these points, we respectfully suggest our earlier assertion that client contacts are the most effective form of positioning. We advise – in almost all cases – that it is better to save your time and money and invest it in client contacts to position for a future procurement.

We recognize that some clients expect to see your firm "get into the hunt" before awarding a new firm a prize. You may have to pay your dues by submitting a few proposals until the client gets comfortable enough to trust you with a small project, but that type of positioning involves truly engaging with the procurement, putting your best foot forward, rather than "throwing" a cobbled-together proposal into the ring.

Capture Plans

Capture plans go hand-in hand with positioning, and help you enhance and protect your marketing investments. These have many names – some firms refer to them as pursuit plans or campaign strategies. It is important to document in writing your approach to positioning. It is easy to forget the details of even the simplest plans with the competing pressure of so many other responsibilities. Written capture plans protect your investment in the event of the loss or transition of key members of the team. Such changes are likely to occur over the course of major pursuits which can take a year or more to unfold. Successive updates keep all team members up to date. Some firms require management review of capture plans, which can serve as the vehicle for approval for further investment, and whether to even propose, or engage in exploring the opportunity at all.

Checklist of capture plan content
1. Client information
2. Project background, understanding, drivers, issues, challenges
3. Potential technical approaches
4. Alternative solutions
5. Selection process description and selection criteria
6. Selection committee members, additional decision-makers
7. Project organization, key staff, teaming partners
8. Firm strengths and weaknesses
9. Competition assessment
10. Proposed competitive strategy with proofs
11. Action items, meetings, client contacts, technical development tasks

Attachments
1. Client contact reports
2. Notes from brainstorming sessions and capture plan meetings
3. Running list of questions to be asked of the client, and responses
4. Key references, reports
5. Marketing budget, schedule

Marketers are ideal facilitators of capture plan development. They tend to focus more on the issues important to winning the pursuit, and not get distracted with technical details. The best facilitators are those who allow the technical details to be discussed and resolved, but who have a low threshold for swerving off onto technical tangents.

Implementing Capture Plans

Positioning activities should be managed as if they were projects. For those with background or experience in project management techniques, this approach should be second nature. There are some valuable project management tools that can be effective in keeping pursuits on track.

As stated in our previous discussions of client contacts, it is helpful to proactively schedule client meetings for technical professionals. These can be calendared and readily displayed for pursuit team members, along with pursuit meetings, brainstorming sessions, site tours, meetings with teaming partners, and management briefings.

Resource allocation and commitment are key. We urge the marketing team to work with management to prioritize pursuit assignments in concert with other responsibilities of the technical professional staff. We always hear of the challenges of finding time for marketing, in freeing up the right people to see clients; these are real challenges. Regularly scheduled pursuit meetings are helpful for resource allocation, revisiting positioning events, making assignments, monitoring results, and establishing accountability.

A Final Note About Positioning

There are many techniques for determining the cost of a pursuit. A "back of the envelope" forecast of the number of people involved in the pursuit, and the length of time they will be involved, can give you a sense for costs. These approximate calculations should be sufficient to give you a sense for the cost of a given pursuit in proportion to other ongoing pursuits, or in comparison to your marketing budget as a whole. Most firms will evaluate pursuit budgets only for the largest investments. Marketing costs can add up quickly and leave you with a nasty surprise if not monitored. If it appears there is too much money being spent, then adjustments should be made to release or downsize resources being applied to the pursuit.

You may be faced with a tough decision, such as halting a costly pursuit when the odds of winning fall below your comfort level. The most important point you may ever learn, pulling the plug on a poor pursuit to focus resources on a better opportunity, may be one of the most important "business decisions" your firm makes to control your marketing destiny.

> *For several weeks, it was amazing to see the effort directed to virtually every aspect of the RFP. Members of the team were dispatched to meet with client staff, to understand the issues, and noodle over potential solutions. Relationships were reinforced and improved. Inevitably, there were some cold calls with folks who weren't well known. Through positioning, the team was able to ferret out key issues missed by the competition, which ultimately became the strengths for our team, and severe weaknesses for the other firm.*
>
> *At the end of the effort, our firm won. Perhaps the most telling anecdote of the success is that we anticipated every question asked by the selection committee during the interview, and had prepared a graphic poster to support each of our responses.*
>
> *Reflecting back on the experience, not only did our leader prevail, but he also taught a generation of future marketers how to ply the craft of positioning for major opportunities.*

Chapter 5
Understanding Selection Processes

"As soon as questions of will or decision or reason or choice of action arise, human science is at a loss."
- *Noam Chomsky, American linguist, philosopher, cognitive scientist*

We often debrief clients to question them about their process for selecting technical professional services firms. Most often, their process involves requesting statements of qualifications, shortlisting a few "qualified" firms, then asking for detailed proposals. After reviewing the documents, they invite a smaller group of firms deemed "most" qualified to attend an interview. Though the procurement processes are often very similar, they always lead to varied outcomes. We are constantly reminded that understanding the nuances of human decision-making is central to being successful.

Earlier, we underscored the importance of preparing for a pursuit through positioning and developing competitive strategies. We now focus on the little (and not so little) things that must be done well in order to win. It is crucial to develop an understanding of the dynamics of selection processes.

You may be wondering, "Why all the fuss? Don't our skills, talent and technology speak for themselves?" We wish they did, but the solutions you and your competitors provide to clients often look and sound the same to them. The art of selling is rooted in the human emotions that are involved in decision-making. These are driven by hopes, fears, likes, dislikes, experience, and personal preference. Technology certainly matters, but it is insufficient. Getting to know people is key to mastering the art of winning.

Formal and Informal Selection Processes

There are two primary types of selection processes: informal and formal. Both are common in the marketplace and can be compared and contrasted:

- Informal. Over a handshake across a desk, a client makes up their mind to award work to a firm. Just like that! Clients of all types often request a scope of work and fee estimate, negotiate the details, and then present a contract to the firm. Sounds simple. However, make no mistake, there was active decision-making by the client, even if they did not request competing bids or proposals. These events have typically followed weeks or months of active positioning by a technical professional marketer. Informal awards may begin as a small assignment to test a firm's performance. If satisfied, the client may reward the firm with increasingly larger assignments. Private companies use this method most often, because they may not be bound by regulated procurement processes.

- Formal. The client solicits for firms to compete for an assignment, asking for information regarding their expertise, then selecting one to be awarded the work. The most common solicitation is an RFQ/RFP (Request for Qualifications and /or Proposals), the creation of which is discussed in detail in The Mechanics of Proposal Production. Many clients request a series of increasingly specific hurdles, such as Qualifications, then Proposals, then Interviews, then perhaps even BAFOs (Best and Final Offers). Often, each hurdle is separated by a selection process that decreases the number of competing firms, until there is only one (or perhaps more than one, in the case of multiple contract awards). Most large, competitive procurements, especially for regulated government contracts, involve these types of multi-step processes.

To us, the overall marketing and business development approach is the same for both informal and formal selection processes; one process simply lacks proposals. They both rely on positive relationships, careful strategies that differentiate one firm from all others, and proven value. Both types of processes build a solid understanding of upcoming engagements through day-to-day dialogue with their customers. In this manner, almost every project (public or private) can be foreseen and can be won through proactive positioning and developing competitive strategies.

Formal Selection Process Steps

Our focus in this chapter is on the complexities of the formal selection process; the informal process was best addressed in our Chapter on Positioning. Formal selection processes often consist of multiple steps, each with their own unique challenges. These can include:

RFLOI – Request for Letters of Interest. Also referred to as *Sources Sought* in Federal government procurements, Letters of Interest are used to gauge interest in a project. An RFLOI is typically issued to the entire universe of technical service providers, though sometimes the invitation focuses on a finite number of firms. In almost all cases, a simple response registers a firm on a list to receive future, more detailed, solicitations. By issuing an RFLOI, a client can contend that they did not exclude any firm from the competition.

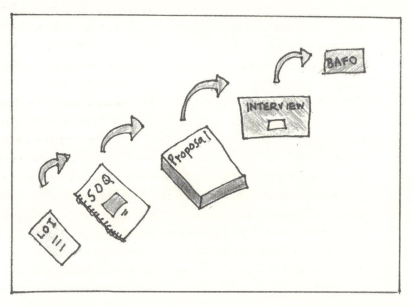

Our mantra: If you're first learning of an opportunity upon reading an RFLOI, you're late to the party. We guarantee that someone else has been positioning for quite some time. A No Go decision at this point will save your staff many hours of effort which could be devoted to positioning for a better opportunity. Also, fully realize that once you pass through this stage, you may be less likely to No Go the pursuit. The reason: you are emotionally and financially invested. There are many (otherwise reasonable) people who say, "Let's just send in a letter of interest, while we figure out the project. It'll only take a marketing coordinator a few hours to prepare." This is the point of no return for many teams; they will continue to use the same logic ("We came this far; might as well keep going. We've already spent $100k, what's another $100k? We have as good a chance as anyone.") This is truly the stage that separates controlled sales programs from crap shoots.

Strategies for successfully passing through the Letter of Interest stage:

- See the "request for a letter of interest" for what it really is: the first breeze in an impending hurricane of effort. It sounds so simple, just a letter, two pages at the most. But pursuing the project can ultimately require many thousands of dollars of effort. Don't make the decision lightly, and don't leave the decision to people you do not trust.
- On the other end of the spectrum, investing a week or two on this process is an obscene waste of time, because clients will not be selecting a firm on the basis of these letters. If you have that sort of time on your hands, instead spend half a day preparing interview slides, so you're more prepared once you're in the heat of battle.
- Assuming you have positioned yourself for this pursuit, and have created a capture plan, then presumably you have developed differentiators. Get them in the letter. Surprisingly, many people prefer to withhold information "in case a client passes our great ideas to a competitor." Our response: you should know the client well enough to ferret out this overwhelming preference for another firm. It is truly rare that a client would put their job at risk by passing information to a competitor. Don't let paranoia rule your business development decisions.
- Assess whether you have a marketing system that can prepare this letter efficiently. 1) are the right people making timely decisions, 2) can your marketing staff communicate the company's differentiators, 3) do you have a database that simplifies the gathering of appropriate information, 4) are your resumes up-to-date? If a Letter of Interest is difficult to produce, it is a sign of an inefficient operation.

RFQ – Request for Qualifications. An RFQ may be used to solicit Statements of Qualifications (SOQ) from which the client will create a shortlist of firms to receive an RFP (Request for Proposals) for a specific project. Second, an RFQ may also be used for formation of a "standing short list" which identifies a roster of firms for future work. RFQs solicit general information about the firm, its capabilities, experience, and key personnel. Sometimes, additional background data are requested, such as proposed subconsultants, financial statements, insurance certifications, or other representations of compliance with client policies.

This is an intermediate step, no ultimate decisions will likely be made here— most of the time. Our mantra: know how your client is defining their process! We can't tell you how many times we've seen firms blindsided by a selection made by the client at this point in the procurement. "We figured we would be invited to submit a proposal, and then make a presentation to really show our stuff." Don't get caught in this type of misunderstanding.

Many people ask, "Why not cut to the chase and request a final proposal from every interested firm?" The answer is: to promote competition. There are many types and sizes of projects: from simple studies to multi-billion dollar, decades-long projects. These procurements can take years and millions of dollars to develop. For clients, it's a delicate process to "entice" candidates, then "reject" those that are unqualified or too expensive. If clients proceed too quickly, they won't attract enough competition.

Strategies for successfully passing through the Qualifications stage:
- Though this is just one part of a possible multi-step selection process, keep in mind your Return on Investment (ROI). You should develop an ability to estimate the anticipated cost (and time) for each step of a procurement. Most firms have an underlying mindset that "we will spend whatever it takes" (see the critical importance of Go/No Go). In fact, you should budget your pursuits in the same manner as your projects, then invest your time and money where it provides the most benefit. The qualifications stage generally is not as critical as the Interview stage. Therefore, you should budget more time and resources for the latter stage. But can you think of a pursuit in which your team spent weeks developing the perfect quals package, then were rushed to develop and practice the interview? We can!

- Again, develop a marketing team that can efficiently create an SOQ with easy to read descriptions of previous experience, concise resumes, and an appealing cover letter. Technical staff should be billing to projects or meeting with clients—they shouldn't be writing cover letters for SOQs. If you employ marketing staff who can't write, you're not an optimized team.
- What is the client looking for within the covers of an SOQ? Clients are measuring the relevance of your past experience against their proposed project. So, show your past performance that most closely matches their project. If it differs in fundamental ways, explain why it is still relevant (in one sentence at the beginning of the description). More about this in the next section on Selection Criteria.
- They are looking for a reason why the technical people you are proposing are the best choice to work with the client's team. "Because they are qualified" is not a reason. "Because they have 25 years of experience" is also not a reason. "Because they have recent experience exceeding the expectations of a nearby client with very similar needs" is a compelling reason because of proof. There is no better qualification than showing an ability to satisfy a client. A reference who can attest to your skills in client satisfaction is the most persuasive information you can provide. A quote from them within the document is a good way to convince the reader to call your reference.

RFP – Request for Proposals. This is the cornerstone solicitation for the procurement of technical services. Thousands of trained writers, coordinators, and graphic designers owe their livelihood to this procurement step. This is such an important element of the sales process that our Chapter on The Mechanics of Proposal Production is devoted to strategies for effectively responding to RFPs.

RFPs ask for detailed, project-specific information, such as a method of approach, scope of work, schedule, and perhaps a fee estimate. In cases where an RFQ did not precede an RFP, qualifying information is also requested in the proposal.

Producing proposals that respond to RFPs represents the bulk of the business development investment of most firms. Clients who are sympathetic to that investment, as well as being guarded of their own time in reading and evaluating submittals, attempt to streamline the selection process by limiting the material they request or the pages allowed in a response. These methods rarely limit the investment of the technical services firm, and sometimes increase it. We can vouch for the fact that it takes more time to write five concise pages of text than 25 pages of free-flowing response. (This is because an open-ended response requires no discipline.)

Responding teams typically are required to invest time in performing enough of the technical work to be able to prepare a credible response to an RFP. This may require significant hours from people in numerous departments. This investment is taken directly away from billable work or from other marketing efforts; it is the most important reason to get the Go/No Go decision right—only invest time in pursuits you have a very good chance of winning. Every hour devoted to a low probability pursuit is one that is stolen away from one of higher probability.

Though we believe it is inherently challenging for a client to select a technical services firm based solely on an evaluation of a written proposal, many selections are made at this stage of the procurement process.

<u>Interviews</u>. It is common for clients to request face-to-face interviews with shortlisted firms. We believe this is where most decisions are really made. It is human nature to want to look someone in the eye and be persuaded. Clients are seeking people they can trust. At the interview, your staff has the opportunity to tell potential clients why they are the best choice for a project. Because of the importance of interviews to the marketing process, our Chapter on Winning Presentations and Interviews offers strategies for addressing this step in the selection process.

The length of an interview can range from 15 minutes to a couple hours. In rare cases, for very large procurements, interviews may last several days. An interview is commonly divided into two elements: a formal presentation of the team's proposal followed by questions and answers. Clients almost always provide specific guidelines for the content of the presentation, and may also offer written questions to be addressed.

One wrinkle is for the client to hand the interview team a set of instructions for presentation content at the beginning of the interview, then be provided a brief amount of time to prepare. We've seen interviews in which the team is handed blank poster paper and markers to develop makeshift graphics. The intent of the selection committee in these cases is to create an environment in which they can view a team's behavior under stress. Be sure to find out if this will be the case *before* you get to the interview. Prepare for possible questions, along with an idea of the graphics you want to create during the interview.

<u>BAFO – Best and Final Offer</u>. In some cases, firms may be provided an opportunity to present a refined price proposal, known as a Best and Final Offer (BAFO), for procurements where prices have been requested. It may not be allowed in many types of Federal procurements where the Brooks Act or other regulations apply. Where we see this element being used most often is for alternative delivery projects that involve program or operations management, design-build, construction, or implementation of information technology systems.

Some of the most valuable people in an organization that win cost proposals are the cost estimators. They have sharpened their pencils through years of experience in construction; they have creative minds that gravitate toward cost-saving ideas; they have nerves of steel that can wait until the last seconds of a procurement deadline to obtain the best bids from subcontractors who are nervous about losing out on the work. And they know just what number will win the work by underbidding their competitors without leaving money on the table. Cheers to the unsung estimators!

Selection Criteria

The solicitations described in this chapter demand that clients sift through vast amounts of information. From all this data, they must select a preferred technical services firm. "Selection criteria" are used to provide a structure for evaluating one firm from another.

> **Menu**
> - Qualifications
> - Organization and Key Personnel
> - Project Understanding
> - Method of approach
> - Schedule
> - Cost, level of effort, best value
> - Capacity to perform
> - Small, disadvantaged business participation
> - Representations and certifications

The basis on which clients make selections is the heart and soul of a firm's sales strategy. The actions of every business developer and marketer involved in formal, competitive pursuits should be focused on these criteria and how they are implemented by the decision-makers.

Selection criteria are sometimes directly stated in the request for proposals from the client. Often, one must deduce the method of selection, based on the information that is requested or from careful discussion with the client. One of the most important skills developed by experienced marketers is the "art of reading an RFP." Here are a few noteworthy examples:

- If the RFP does not state the method by which the client will select a firm, one can deduce the intent of the client by the amount and relative proportions of information they request. For example, if the RFP requests significant detail on project performance, but very little on your staff, you can surmise that the client is most interested in a firm that has "done it before." Of course, you should know the client's interests based on your positioning.
- If the RFP asks for specific references for your proposed staff, rather than for the firm in general, it's a sign that they're more interested in the people they will be working with, rather than the reputation of the company.
- If the RFP has exacting page limits and font requirements, it's a sign that the process is in the hands of a procurement department, rather than the technical staff. This creates a buffer between the client and the service provider and can make it harder to decipher the intent of the document. It's also a sign that the client has been burned by contract protests, so they are extremely vigilant about "fairness." This is where talented marketers help a firm to follow the exact letter of the RFP.

Let's describe some of the most common selection categories from which clients attempt to differentiate one firm from another.

<u>Qualifications</u>. Qualifications consist of company capabilities and experience, which are used to differentiate "qualified" from "unqualified" firms. Clients use this differentiator to develop shortlists of firms by weeding out those with no history of successfully completing similar work. Competency in the required services is the first step in developing credibility with the client.

Potential technical services firms are challenged to describe their past performance in a way that details similarities to the proposed project. Good marketers take care to tailor their project descriptions with this in mind, rather than carelessly pasting together boilerplate. Proposers also should be prepared to offer references from past clients who are willing to vouch for the firm.

A key question is, "How do you break into a new service area? If clients only want firms who have performed similar projects, there is seemingly no way to win a project unless you've already done it before." We have seen cases in which firms have been selected for work of a type or magnitude that they have not performed previously. There are a couple of strategies to meet this challenge:

- Divide the challenge into smaller steps. For example, if your goal is to win the design of regional hospitals, then winning a series of smaller health care facilities will support a strategy of "graduating" to larger ones.
- Team with a firm (or hire a person) who has the experience, gaining it by association.
- Perform pre-design of the project in your proposal, proving to the client that you have the skills.

> *Never take references for granted. Always verify directly with the client that you have permission to use their name. This accomplishes several things.*
>
> *First, seeking permission provides a proper level of respect. Particularly for sensitive or confidential assignments, you cannot assume that the client is willing to discuss your work with others.*
>
> *Second, you're alerting the client to be prepared for a phone call or written request for information. Clients are busy, and they will be more receptive, if forewarned.*
>
> *Third, you're checking to ensure that the reference will be favorable. Don't laugh – we've seen many cases where the reference's response was not complimentary. Weak or unfavorable references can easily result from staff being unaware of the perspective of the caller.*
>
> *Also, there's nothing worse than providing incorrect telephone numbers, addresses, or citing the name of a person who is no longer at the organization.*
>
> *Finally, ask the reference to call you after they are contacted. You will learn a lot from the questions they were asked.*

Qualifications can't be "fudged," but they can be nuanced and presented to the client (especially through meetings, while you are positioning for the project) in a way that leverages past experience.

<u>Project organization and key personnel</u>. The project organization criterion asks proposers to define the roles and responsibilities of the people who will accomplish the work. In addition, you may be requested to provide a management plan for organizing and directing these people.

Obviously, for simple projects, the organization chart should be simple, commensurate with the scope and budget. For more complicated projects, a more complex organization may be required to ensure that all of the project's technical needs are covered. In addition, lines of reporting must be identified. Key personnel should be identified based on your competitive strategy, rather than on availability.

Assign staff for project controls and quality assurance, as well as senior staff for value-added advisory functions. The project organization should also consider all phases of the client's assignment, from planning to design to construction, for example. Even though the RFP is only addressing a primary phase, you should be positioning for the remaining parts of the assignment.

The savvy marketer also designs the project organization chart with due consideration for who will be attending a formal interview. While some clients may recoil at this notion, nothing hamstrings a sales process more than having superior technical staff members that do not have interviewing skills. You put them on the org chart, because they have a terrific resume, but you have a sinking feeling that, when shortlisted to interview, they won't be able to convince a client to select your firm.

The organization chart is a key element to present and "pre-sell" to the client before you submit your proposal. Their impression when seeing it at a meeting (of course, this is prior to release of the RFP) will tell you a lot about your teaming strategy, your choice of project manager, and your level of staffing. This is a critical step in positioning.

As a word of caution, we stress that proposed key personnel be prepared to engage in the work, if selected. Clients will consider any attempt to "bait and switch" proposed staff to be a breach of trust. Indeed, we see clients increasingly binding names of key personnel into contracts, in order to prevent this behavior (as a breach of *contract*).

Project understanding. Many RFPs ask proposers to present their understanding of the engagement. This permits firms to showcase their perspective of the project and the challenges to be faced. The narrative should feature a grasp of the key issues, both known to the client, as well as those they may not be aware of. This portion of the proposal is an ideal place to show your ability to communicate effectively to a wide audience (shorthand for not boring readers with pages of technical information). Liberal use of charts, graphs, and tables will engage readers and convey detailed technical information in the fewest number of pages.

Method of approach. Your approach to meeting the client's needs should be the heart of your proposal. Your writing should walk the client through the sequence of events and flow of tasks. Each activity should be specific to the client's needs, not generalized or pasted from previous proposals. Where applicable, discuss the advantages and disadvantages of certain methodologies to illustrate the value of your ideas. Flow charts or other diagrams are helpful for visualizing the sequence of events and interrelationships of tasks (these will also be useful during the interview).

Offering proof of the value of your ideas, based on experience with other clients, is of utmost importance. Systematically demonstrating that you have succeeded in similar challenges in the past will help build confidence with the client. Proofs can take many forms – sometimes a simple photograph of a completed project will say it all. Tables that present financial results, or abbreviated case studies, can also be helpful. Of course, a glowing client testimonial is the ultimate proof of past performance.

A question often asked, "Is there a danger of presenting too much forethought of a solution to their problem? Won't the client want their ideas included?" Our answer: Yes, exactly. Nothing in your project approach (in fact nothing in your proposal) should be a surprise to them. During positioning, you should have collaborated with the client to develop a working approach to the project that includes all they know about the issues. If your potential client is unwilling to share information of this nature with you, ask yourself if they are a client you want to work with. And remember, after the RFP is released, most clients CANNOT talk to you at this desired level of detail. So, this must be done beforehand. Hence, our constant question: why would anyone pursue a project for which they have not positioned?

Schedule. Deadlines are important to clients. Accordingly, RFPs often request a timeline of the flow of tasks. In the simplest form, horizontal (GANTT) bar charts meet the need of identifying time frames for each major task, along with important milestones. As the complexity of the project grows, the proposer may use sophisticated software to generate schedules, such as Microsoft Project or Primavera Project Planner. These software packages also offer tools for evaluating critical path, resource loading, and cash flow projection.

One observation we would make is that we often find schedules dumped into a proposal without any discussion of the reasoning behind the overall concept or its details. Not supplying your approach to meeting deadlines may cost you points, especially if a competitor presents an insightful discussion of their own schedule.

A talented visual artist can create diagrams or other depictions of the sequence of events that "speak" to clients. The intent is to convince the client of your ability to communicate complex information in a simple form. A 1,000 line schedule may be "accurate," but will communicate far less effectively than a graphic summary that can be instantly comprehended. This is especially important for non-technical decision-makers.

<u>Cost, level of effort, best value</u>. Many RFPs request an estimated cost for the project. Sometimes, only a rate schedule is requested. In some locales, requesting price for professional services in a proposal is illegal, including Federal work conducted under the Brooks Act.

In almost all cases, the client will request a breakdown of the scope of services by task, with an estimated level of effort by personnel classification. In addition to professional labor, other costs will be requested for expenses, such as travel, office equipment, computer aided design services, and communications. In addition, proposers are also likely to be asked for specific charges unique to your own method of cost accounting. It is important to keep in mind the difference between cost, price and value (covered more under our Chapter on Closing the Deal). Pricing should include profit, whereas cost is your raw cost, including overhead for labor and expenses.

In addition, best value is increasingly becoming a selection criterion for clients who consider not only price, but also the overall final life-cycle cost of the finished project. This usually applies to full-scale implementation of new information technology systems, or construction of operating facilities. These clients recognize that capital or initial costs are often smaller than the recurring costs for operating a facility.

<u>Capacity to perform</u>. This criterion tends to apply to larger or more complex projects. The client is looking for evidence that your firm is large enough and has sufficient resources to accomplish the scope of work within the required time. Responding to this would be simple if clients weren't aware that your firm has other projects and commitments. You may be asked to show your available bandwidth overlaid on top of other commitments. In our experience, you should take this seriously and be as accurate as possible. It is surprisingly easy for clients to check whether you are faking the data. Clients talk to one another; they frequently will be aware of other projects being conducted by your firm. As mentioned previously,

many scheduling software packages offer tools for resource loading which are helpful, especially as they can present the information graphically.

Small and/or disadvantaged business participation. Increasingly, public clients will require targets for including small or disadvantaged businesses on teams. This almost is a uniform requirement for Federal government procurements. Quite often, you'll be presented with forms to complete which satisfy this criterion (or to show a "good faith effort" to comply). If you are able to present proof of past compliance (or better yet, exceeding minimum levels), then this can be a differentiator. Agencies that establish these programs typically assign individuals to manage compliance. They will look at one thing in your proposal– this section. We have seen cases where this criterion is not evaluated based on points, but rather a pass/fail grade for your entire proposal.

Representations and certifications. This category includes many of the procedural requirements of solicitations. The most common elements include:

- Contract compliance. Increasingly, clients are attaching contracts to RFPs, asking for comments or a certification that your firm is willing to accept the contract "as is." We don't like this approach very much because negotiation of contracts through a proposal (which is a sales document) does not seem fair. Also, we are suspect of clients who adopt a "take it or leave it" attitude with their technical service providers. The best advice we can offer is to propose contract changes, stressing the benefit to the client or reasonable justification for your position. You may be asked to furnish a track record of your firm's litigation or claims history, as well. Your firm's Chief Counsel or Chief Administrative Officer is your best friend in responding to this criterion.

- Conformance with policies, law. Some clients request certification for compliance with a wide variety of their own policies, and in some cases laws or local ordinances. We have seen items ranging from offering benefits to domestic partners of employees to compliance with living wage ordinances. Also common is compliance with equal employment opportunity regulations, breakdown of racial and/or national origin of proposed staff, as well as number of staff residing within the City limits.

- Insurance certifications. These are routinely requested during contract negotiations, but we also see this incorporated into RFPs.

As clients become increasingly averse to risk, we predict there will be more need to attach proof of insurance forms to proposals. Our recommendation is to be diligent; these items won't win a project, but could easily cause you to lose.

We once performed three debriefs, back to back, after our firm was selected for a string of projects. Though each project was very different, the same word was used at every meeting. At about the same point in the conversation, after talking about the particularities of their procurement process, we felt a need to clarify the critical factor in our selection over other qualified firms. "Why us," we asked? Each client looked around the room, trying to find the right word. Each said the same thing: "Enthusiasm. You guys seemed most excited about the prospect of working on the project."

We were dumbfounded. Not that it wasn't gratifying to hear that we had successfully communicated our excitement at the prospect of working with the client. But rather, in all the pages of the RFP, and all of the selection criteria, how would we know that enthusiasm was the most important factor? We knew then that being selected for a project would always involve human emotions— an important realization when engaged in a selection that seems to be a "technical" process.

Chapter 6
The Dynamics of Selection Committees

"Making good decisions is a crucial skill at every level."
- Peter Drucker, Author, professor, management consultant

We pursued a construction management assignment for a new water treatment plant. The team developed a terrific proposal and interview. The selection committee ranked us number one, and they passed along their recommendation to their governing body to award us a contract.

This was a highly contested pursuit; unfortunately, a competitor who was not selected began to communicate directly with members of the governing body. They passed along some untruths about our firm, suggesting that we were from a State over 2,000 miles away. (In reality, our office was a 45 minute drive from the project site). Also, one member of the governing body had recently tangled with us over a messy contract issue, leaving both individuals with bruises. We were afraid the governing body would overturn the selection committee's recommendation, leaving us empty-handed after a lengthy and costly pursuit.

It all comes down to the decision-makers-- thumbs-up or thumbs-down. For technical services firms in competitive environments, it is critical to know the people who select us for projects. Many clients allow individual managers to make buying decisions. In those cases, our task is to convince that manager to select us. This formidable activity is covered in our chapter on Relationships. However, when presented with a need to make major decisions involving large capital expenditures, most clients will form a committee. This is based on the natural desire to create consensus, gain buy-in, and spread risk.

Selection committees consist of decision-makers who hold your destiny in their hands. Their interpretation and subsequent deliberation of your competitive strategies, messages, and proofs will carry the day. Despite the specific selection criteria stated in their procurement documents, the experiences, personal preferences, hopes, and fears of the committee members will come into play in reaching a decision. They are human, after all, and they are all making "personal" decisions.

In our experience, we've seen all sorts of methods to reach a decision, such as selection committees deciding between competitors based on developing reasons "not to select" one over the other (that's why capable firm's proposals are sometimes thrown out on technicalities, such as page count or font size, allowing the one submittal that passes all barriers to be the "selected" contestant). It's a fascinating view of human psychology.

In fact, it is this dynamic which accentuates the *art* in selling *rocket science*. As you get to know individual members, and drill down below the project technical issues into their hopes and fears, likes and dislikes, you begin to appreciate how science fades into the background as selection committee members deliberate over a decision. Compounding the challenge is the group dynamic within selection committees as they interact. Personalities clash, ring-leaders emerge. This uncertainty differentiates the art from the science of our technical business.

Types of Selection Committees

Though you would like to think of the committee as a single unit, the vast majority of them are far from homogeneous; they are comprised of unique individuals, each with their own view of the world. This increases the challenge to the marketer. The pursuit leaders are tasked with persuading the majority of the committee members on the advantages of one firm over all others—knowing that committee members may have competing individual selection criteria. We have found patterns in the combinations of groups that are formed into selection committees, which are worth discussing to gain an appreciation for the challenge:

- Typical. If there is such a thing as a typical selection committee, it would consist of 3-5 members, of fairly equal rank within the client organization, led by the project manager in charge of the assignment. The leader might also be a middle-manager with a technical background. The key to winning: position with each member.
- Boss sits in. The simplest variation on the typical committee is when a supervisor or director of a department joins in. Even when this person is not a "voting member," they influence the rest of the members. Almost always, the boss has authority to approve or disapprove of the committee's recommendation. The key to winning: make sure you have the boss' vote. If you don't, it might not matter that you have all the other votes.
- Outsider invited. Peers from other departments or organizations are sometimes invited to join in the selection process to add expertise or to balance discussions. They may or may not have a vote. These outsiders often have less of an understanding of the proposed project, and may have other priorities. The key to winning: Get to know the outsider, if possible, but don't over-shift your strategy for them; they likely have little influence.
- All outsiders. We see occasions where agencies will organize selection groups comprised completely of outsiders. This may seem surprising at first, but it is often a defensive measure on the part of staff to avoid criticism over impartiality. It also validates a contention that some clients see shortlisted firms as being more or less equal, and that they could "live with" the selection of any firm. The key to winning: Keep your technical strategy simple; this group likely will have a limited understanding of the project.

- <u>Very large</u>. Some selection committees can reach 10 or more members. Frequently, these groups include outsiders, specialist advisors, and elected officials. Obviously, it is impossible to appeal to all members, as agreement on a topic by a group that size is difficult. The challenge here is to identify the most influential people in the group, while being mindful of the special interests represented by the others. As a side note, the leadership strength of the selection committee chair becomes an important issue, as does the system by which they will vote (more on that later).
- <u>Open meeting</u>. Some governmental agencies conduct technical professional consultant interviews in a public meeting. This not only means that the world is invited to observe, but so are your competitors. Your messages, strategies, and responses to questions will be "out there," so care must be taken with proprietary ideas and sensitive issues. At the same time, you'll be afforded a golden opportunity to watch your competitors as they make their pitch.
- <u>Presence of political official(s)</u>. These include representatives from a governing board of an organization, Board of Directors, City Council members, or other elected/appointed officials. If the selection committee consists of one or more political decision-makers, then three potential conditions may be true. First, the decision will be political, otherwise the politicians would not invest their time. Second, the selection will be weighted toward non-technical criteria. Third, the other members of the selection committee will defer to the politicians. The key to winning: know the politics.
- <u>Presence of staff advisor(s)</u>. Staff representation can include a procurement officer, small or disadvantaged business program coordinator, health and safety manager, and many types of operations staff. Often, these individuals are responsible for validating a single issue, such as compliance with a specific proposal requirement, awarding a grade of pass/fail. Therefore, these people can rarely help you, but they can hurt you, so you need to meet their needs.
- <u>Presence of consultant advisor(s)</u>. Hired advisors are sometimes present at the request of the selection committee to offer advice on complex topics outside of the specialty of the members. As a

hired gun, they'll be listened to, but they may not have a vote. In many cases, the hired consultant will be retained not only for technical advice, but also could be managing or coordinating the selection process. In our experience, because advisors are paid handsomely, the committee wants to get its money's worth, so they listen attentively to their advice, no matter how low value it may really be. The key to winning: treat these advisors as if they were full-fledged decision-makers.

An obvious question is, "does the makeup of the selection committee really matter?" The answer is, absolutely yes. We think the average pursuit team spends too little time thinking about their audience. How can you possibly persuade people if you don't even know who they are?

How Committees Make Decisions

No matter the selection system a committee uses, you will be judged against your peers. Understanding how human nature plays into the process, and how clients with technical backgrounds attempt to use numerology to reach decisions, are important elements of the sales process.

It is quite common for committees charged with selecting a technical services provider to use a spreadsheet or matrix scoring system. These types of scoring systems are meant to diligently apply procurement rules to achieve fair and objective decisions. There are as many scoring systems as stars in the sky. In the example provided below, three members of a selection committee judge three competitors using five weighted criteria.

Sample Spreadsheet Scoring System

Criteria	Weight
Project Understanding	10%
Project Team	30%
Method of Approach	30%
Related Experience	20%
Capacity to Perform	10%
Total	100%

Member 1	Firm A	Firm B	Firm C
Project Understanding	7	8	8
Project Team	8	7	8
Method of Approach	9	8	9
Related Experience	9	8	9
Capacity to Perform	7	9	9
Member 1 Score	8.3	7.8	8.6

Member 2	Firm A	Firm B	Firm C
Project Understanding	8	9	8
Project Team	7	8	8
Method of Approach	8	7	8
Related Experience	8	7	8
Capacity to Perform	9	8	9
Member 2 Score	7.8	7.6	8.1

Member 3	Firm A	Firm B	Firm C
Project Understanding	7	8	6
Project Team	8	7	8
Method of Approach	9	8	8
Related Experience	9	8	7
Capacity to Perform	7	9	6
Member 3 Score	8.3	7.8	7.4
Average Scores	8.1	7.7	8.0

The example shows that even well-intentioned selection committee members can end up making unexpected choices. If we look only at the rankings of the first two members of the committee, the math shows they selected Firm C with scores of 8.6 and 8.1. However, knowingly (or unknowingly), Member 3 controlled the selection because his or her votes for Firm C were a little lower, enough to drop the average, so that Firm A was ranked number one, **even though two of three members rated Firm C higher!** Anyone can readily see how an average is lowered by a slight drop in the raw scores. But the point is (this is important to understand) you aren't playing a game of chance, you are working with a complex system with many variables.

More thoughtful selection committees conduct a closer examination of the ordinal scoring, especially for a close finish. This often results in some questioning of the committee's own decision-making criteria. There are some additional insights to be gained from the example.

- The bandwidth of scoring is often quite narrow, even where the overall range is large (so we see many 6s, 7s, 8s, and 9s out of a range of 1-10). This is a convergence of two phenomena, the first being that competitors tend to be seen as equivalent in qualifications. There is a lot to be learned from this, but the most significant is the importance of being different AND being memorable. The second phenomenon is that many selection committee members are polite (nice individuals trying to do the right thing). They wouldn't dream of scoring someone less than 5 on a scale of 1-10. As a result, scores tend to be bunched. Both observations are imperatives for marketers developing winning strategies. Leave nothing to chance!
- In the example, a single individual controlled the decision. This can happen intentionally, or unintentionally, but it doesn't matter. By better understanding the tendencies of selection committee members, and how they vote (based on their behavioral styles), then obtaining a winning vote from the most influential member becomes a top priority.
- If a selection committee begins to question the scoring system, and has a conversation about its value, then they are modifying the procurement process. Some competitors might find this unfair, but in stories told during numerous debriefs, it happens frequently. We've even heard of multiple rounds of scoring, with discussion in between, much like a trial jury deliberating a felony case. Selection committees can become deadlocked, taking hours, even days, to reach a decision. The differentiators between the competing firms can lead the decision-makers far away from their intended selection criteria.

If you're a client, and you apply similar mathematical scoring processes to reach decisions, we hope you're not surprised. Hopefully, this reinforces the notion that not everything can be quantified to make appropriate decisions. Understanding the math is helpful in gaining an appreciation for its weaknesses as a decision-making tool.

Close Calls

Nothing shines a light on the dynamic nature of group-based decision-making more than the "Close Call." Close calls are highly competitive pursuits in which the outcome is based on minor differentiators. Individuals looking to hone their marketing skills should focus on understanding close calls, as they offer more learning experiences than the slam-dunk wins.

In an ironic twist, close calls are sometimes settled over reasons "not to select" a particular firm. This process is opposed to the more expected behavior of selecting a winner based on their strengths. Anticipating and preparing for this type of behavior can dramatically improve your chances of prevailing. In fact, there are a number of tie-breaker strategies which can routinely be applied well in advance, if you anticipate the decision will be "tight."

Value of Close Calls

Business developers by nature are competitors, driven by the need to win, whether the reward is a million dollar project or an undefined, indefinite delivery contract. For many true competitors, the sweetest victories are the photo-finishes. Landslide wins seem less satisfying, and from a learning perspective are far less insightful.

The "too close to call" victory speaks volumes on the nature of the decision-making process. You can learn to identify and anticipate close calls by understanding their characteristics. By evaluating the nature of the decision-making, and the behavior of competitors and judges, you can take action to increase your chances for winning.

In close calls, small things make a big difference. When competitors are evenly matched, seemingly trivial aspects of a proposal or presentation become magnified. Moreover, intangibles such as emotions and other subtleties can become the main differentiators. Clients will often cite "enthusiasm" as the main reason they selected one firm over another.

- <u>Know the scoring system</u>. First and foremost, spend quality time reading the scoring system for the selection process, and consider how criteria are described and/or weighted. In some procurements, these are applied strictly by law (e.g., a Brooks Act Federal procurement).
- <u>Try to win the vote of each selection committee member</u>. If you can't win someone's vote because they have a clear favorite, at least try to place a close second.

- <u>Don't offend anyone</u>. This should go without saying, in trying to win someone's vote, don't throw another selection committee member's vote overboard. This is easily done when the selection committee has diverse views on an issue and your competitive strategy requires you to take a firm stand.
- <u>Apply overwhelming force</u>. Use your strongest assets by picking the best people your company can offer for the project team. Go all out for the proposal. Then go all out again for the interview. Don't hold back. Anticipate that you will be involved in a close call. We often hear in proposal brainstorming, "let's save that idea for the interview." Don't do it. It's an excuse to be lazy at the proposal stage; go all out at every step of the procurement.
- <u>Appeal to known hot buttons</u>. If you've done your homework and know your customer's needs, then focus on meeting them. This is easy to say, and is just as easily ignored. It takes discipline to drill down into a selection committee member's most important points, and then work out responsive solutions.
- <u>Stick to basic factors</u>. Quite often, pursuit teams have good ideas, but stop short of delivering the message. Ideas are presented, without elaboration on the benefit to the client. Benefits should be explained simply, so that our mothers can understand them in a 30-second elevator ride. Moreover, benefits should be articulated in more than one way, so as to appeal to each selection committee member's own specific hot button. Cost can almost never be ruled out.
- <u>Get a cold-eyes review</u>. Such is the purpose of "red teams." This is a big deal, which is to be addressed in more detail in our chapter on proposal production. Over the course of a pursuit, the team can lose perspective by growing too close. An independent team should act as the client's selection committee. This is similar to war games, where the Army has a team acting and thinking as the enemy. A review is an opportunity to critically evaluate your team's strategy. Actively debate and respond to the question, "What will the client say when asked for the reasons why we weren't selected?"
- <u>Avoid rationalization at all costs</u>. It is easy to talk yourself out of doing the hard things. Discuss, vet, and address every issue that you uncover. Quite often, we fall into the trap of saying that the

client has "issues that can't be determined", or we believe that we are in fact weaker and cannot develop a mitigating strategy. These are all rationalizations which could cost the win by allowing a vote to slip.

There is a tendency for technical staff to be infatuated with their own technology. Technical issues can always be offset by non-technical factors. No matter the level of complexity of a project, it pales in comparison with the variations of human emotions involved in decision-making.

The governing body began to question the selection committee's recommendation to select our firm. What were we going to do?

Through associates and colleagues, we reached out to the decision-makers who were raising concerns. A senior vice president got personally involved in these meetings. Through a series of conversations, we systematically addressed each and every concern. Interestingly, at least two members of the governing body remarked that they appreciated our direct approach with them, having grown a little frustrated with early attempts by the selection committee to bar access.

In this manner, we were able to address the untruths and expose the weak claims made by our competitor. We also were fortunate in identifying an additional relationship established at the national level between a governing body member and an employee of our subsidiary company. Once the two old friends made contact, and could see the values of their personal contacts extended to our firm, the controversy was ended.

The governing body voted at their next official meeting to award the contract to our firm.

Chapter 7
The Mechanics of Proposal Production

"A perfect method for adding drama to life is to wait until the deadline looms large."
- Alyce P. Cornyn-Selby, Author, Procrastinator's Success Kit

After a couple years of experience as a marketing coordinator, I remember feeling a bit arrogant. There was one particular proposal to a major city public works department where I wanted to show my stuff. I had a brilliant idea; I ordered special paper with a custom logo printed in color in the footer (yes, this is before color printers, kids).

I had set aside the majority of a day to print 16 copies of the proposal. My vendor was late in delivering the special paper stock. 10:00 AM rolled by, then 11:00. Finally, the paper arrived, and I started production. I did not accurately estimate how long it would take to reproduce the proposal. The document was several hundred pages long, with tabbed dividers and lots of collating. The deadline was 4:00 PM. By 3:30, it was obvious I was not going to make all 16 sets of the document. The copier just wasn't fast enough; I had badly miscalculated. So, at 3:45, we packed up nine copies and dashed down to City Hall, luckily only a few blocks away. When we arrived at the curb, I flung myself out of the car, raced into the grand old City building, charged into the Contracts office, and slammed the box on the counter.

The clerk in the bid and bond room was a corn-fed Chicagoan, as big as a brownstone. He shoved a triplicate receipt in the time-clock, which printed the time on the form with the sound of a gunshot. KACHOW. It read 3:59:42. Yes, it printed the seconds.

So, I made the deadline, barely. But because we had not submitted the correct number of copies, our submittal *was thrown out. Ask me what I think about using fancy paper for proposals. Go ahead, ask me.*

Over the course of our careers, we have written hundreds of proposals. Proposals of all kinds: letter proposals, bid proposals, horribly bad proposals, surprisingly good proposals, one-day turnaround proposals, proposals that took a year to write, federal proposals (SF254/255s, SF330s), sole source proposals. So many proposals that it makes our heads spin. But they all were singular experiences. We can remember nearly every one of them, because a piece of us was left behind in each.

For all types of documents and all services for

> I remember the first proposal I worked on. October 1990. The RFP was straight-forward. Introduction, project experience, project approach, resumes. The project manager was one of the nicest guys you could meet. No drama, no pressure. Even though I'm sure it took me twice as long as he was expecting, I think he was pleased because 1) my work instinct told me to take responsibility for the deadline and the quality of the document, rather than forcing it back on him, and 2) my writing instinct told me that technical writing of this sort was no different than any other writing you want people to read; make the proposal interesting, to the point, and remove the clutter of excess language that buries the messages.

which you are applying, whether its civil engineering, accounting, architecture, or law, the job is the same: persuade a client to select you. Moreover, since many decision-makers do not have technical knowledge (which is why they need a firm like yours), your job is to develop a proposal that captures technical material in a way that non-technical readers can understand.

Technical professionals have an innate desire to explain their thinking process sequentially—task by task, step by step, definable by hour and dollar. The business developer has the job of persuading, rather than explaining. Persuasion aims to connect methodology to a higher level of emotional desirability, speaking to the client's aspirations. This makes the technical staff and the business developer a complementary partnership. Balanced correctly, they work well together; out of balance, they are inefficient and ineffective. <u>The partnership of technical staff and business developer is the critical component of a pursuit team.</u>

Proposal Production is the fulcrum in the balance inherent in the art of selling rocket science. The technical people will be immediately drawn into all of the intricate details of the project; the business developer will be focused on closing the deal. Working together, they balance the equally important need to use complex technical ideas to connect with the emotions of the client.

Once the team forms around the task of writing a winning proposal, the process can either be 1) memorializing an already-established and vetted strategy for meeting the client's needs (if the team is positioned), or 2) the beginning of a "process of a thousand guesses" (if they are not positioned).

If the team has discussed the project with the client in detail, then the proposal should be a document which demonstrates that they have learned a great deal in those conversations. Writing the proposal becomes an act of methodically persuading the client that the team understands the client's desires and has the people, process, and technology to satisfy those desires. If the team is responding to an unanticipated RFP and has not talked to the client privately about it, the team will spend many hours in a conference room, pouring through every word of the RFP, trying to guess what the client is thinking. In the first example, many hours are invested prior to the RFP; in the second, many more hours are spent after its arrival.

We can tell you that we've been at both ends of the spectrum— being perfectly positioned on one end, and responding to unforeseen RFPs on the other. After all these experiences in winning and losing, we've learned two things: 1) the proposal is a part of the sales process, not the entire process; and 2) the proposal is nearer to the end of the timeline of activity during a pursuit, than the beginning.

There are a lot of books on writing proposals, each with their own multi-step process to developing a winning proposal. We will not repeat the points made in those books. We won't take you back through the importance of having a competitive strategy, the advantage of relationships, or the value of positioning. However, the proposal, and subsequent interview, is where a client <u>confirms</u> their decision that you are the preferred firm for them. They almost never choose you if they don't know you prior to their reading your proposal.

Here's our take on the process:
- Confirm your Go decision, verifying your positioning and strategy to win
- Storyboard the interview and the proposal. Build a detailed outline and structure your proposal
- Get organized
- Keep the technical team on track
- Respond to all of the client's requests
- Finish early
- Leave nothing to chance.

Now, in a little detail.

Confirm Your Go Decision

The most expensive proposal is one in which you are not selected, so achieving a high rate of selection saves you the most money in the long run. A rigorous Go/No-Go process places your bet down on a strong hand of cards. Your hit rate will increase and provide you with more resources to bring to projects with greater potential.

It is critical to confirm the Go decision. We explained in an earlier chapter that a Go decision should be a formality upon receipt of the RFP. The operative word here is "should." If you have done your positioning well and have been working on a pursuit for some time, then it should be obvious that you're making a

---

As you have heard us preach, we're opposed to "go" if the RFP was unanticipated, because you will not be positioned. However, in reality, when should it be considered?

1. *Someone in the client's organization coaches you. Or you have a superior relationship with the client and you're asked to submit a proposal.*
2. *You are truly uniquely qualified. This may include having a terrific idea for a solution to the client's problem or expertise only your firm possesses or, better yet, both.*
3. *You and the competition are all caught by surprise, and the playing field is truly level.*

The presence of all of these conditions improves your chances of being successful. We caution that you must be ultra-critical with your strengths to overcome the severe weakness of not knowing the RFP would show up in the mail. Rationalization is an inherent weakness of technical professionals and you must be ruthlessly objective about your chances of winning.

How often would we do this? Allow one "get-out-of-jail-free" per year.

positive decision to write a proposal in response to an anticipated RFP. This is an argument in favor of identifying opportunities early and taking control of your destiny by conducting the activities you need to perform to win.

At the opposite end of the spectrum, an RFP that shows up unanticipated is almost certainly cause for a No Go decision. Between the obvious Go proposal and the obvious No Go is the gray area where positioning wasn't as thorough as it could be, but you want to believe you could win the project. In this gray area, there is room for debate about whether to write a proposal.

The key question to ask yourself when reconfirming the Go decision is: What has changed since your initial discovery of the project? Hopefully, you have advanced your strategy to the client and to your internal team. Here's a test: can your marketing coordinator and your project specialist recite your winning message? If you haven't communicated your message internally, how is your team going to pull together a winning proposal?

From our perspective, the marketer can make a key contribution by expediting a rapid decision. If the chances of winning look poor, then you should be lobbying for the team to drive a stake in the heart of the RFP. The faster you move to a decision, the better your odds of winning because you will have more time. Time spent reaching a Go decision can hurt your prospects of winning during the pursuit phase. Push for a good, fast decision, because time spent on debate is time not spent on the proposal.

We also note that it is important to have buy-in for the pursuit from a few key people, such as management, technical resources needed for the project, and the marketing team. Without support from key individuals, it will be difficult for a proposal to successfully come together. Many people find this to be a little hard to believe, but it is true. Consider the organizational structure of a technical professional services firm. Are the marketers ever in charge, or in control of technical people? Never. So, the marketer's instruments of success are not command and control, rather they are reason, logic, influence and charm. As a marketer, you do not want to be in the position of trying to lead or push through a proposal when even one person disagrees with the pursuit. It's tough enough when they are all universally supportive!

After the Go/No Go decision, it's time to Go-Go-Go. Don't worry about the decision or keep re-deciding. It's often easier to <u>talk</u> about pursuing a pursuit than actually <u>pursuing</u> it. Make a decision, invest your time well, then get organized and move toward resolution.

Storyboard the Interview and the Proposal

Nothing is more a waste of time than spending hours of company time and money slaving away on proposal or interview content that won't help you win. Seem obvious? We wish it were so clear to everyone. We repeatedly see technical professionals who scour the scientific and engineering details of an RFP, then invest hours in search of the perfect solution to the client's problem, but never consider the selection criteria, the competitive strategy, the proofs, theme or messages of a proposal. We wish they would refocus their energy on what matters.

We are not the first people to think of this, but it is immensely helpful to storyboard. Almost nobody wants to do this, but it makes all of the sense in the world. It is simply more efficient to spend a half day laying out potential pages (knowing that you are proceeding correctly), than it is to spend a half day writing part of your technical approach (that may never be used). The intent of storyboarding is to quickly ensure that the products from your positioning efforts and competitive strategy are incorporated into your document as understandable benefits to the client.

Begin by developing a simple outline of your messages, then identify proofs in the form of graphics, tables, or photographs. Draw up each page to show the flow of major headings based on an outline. This forces you to think through the proposal flow and ensures that you do not leave anything out. It allows you to envision the final printed document before actually beginning to write. More importantly, it clearly identifies graphic elements that you can get started on right away, while text is being composed.

Most importantly, if the RFP stipulates a page limit (many do), then you can allocate all pages in your storyboard. A strict page budget can be invaluable in limiting writers to only the amount of text allowed. Considering the page budget in advance will minimize the future agony of cutting treasured text written by well-intended technical professionals.

> In the 70's and 80's, many proposals were typewritten on IBM Selectrics (look it up, kids). Typos were subjected to White Out. In the early nineties, color copiers were developed, but were expensive. I remember running down to the copy shop, making copies of a single sheet of paper (usually a page containing a color or bar chart), then running back upstairs and collating it into the proposal sets. We could only afford and allow time for one color page per proposal. Now, you wouldn't think twice about having a proposal in which every page contains professionally designed color graphics.
>
> The bar has been raised, and clients are the lucky recipients of all this glam. But the mission has always been the same: differentiate yourself!

The storyboarding process boils your ideas and messages into images. These are what will penetrate the minds of the selection committee. The best graphic designers can take the convoluted thoughts of a proposal team and turn them into clearly understood, memorable illustrations that support the competitive strategy, replacing pages of language. Firms without graphic designers draft their marketing coordinators into developing charts and graphs. But there is a world of difference between a graphic developed by a semi-skilled marketer and one by a designer. The best graphic designers are worth their weight in gold (but don't tell them that- it'll go to their head).

And the answer to your question is: yes, pretty pictures win jobs. Everything that sets you apart, and that communicates effectively to your audience will greatly support your competitive strategy. Communicating complex technical information to non-technical people is often required of services firms, and your proposal and presentation are proof of how well you perform.

Get Organized

Two important points of focus for a marketer to contribute to a successful proposal effort:
- Help to clearly articulate your competitive strategy, messages, and proofs, forming a compelling argument that your firm should be selected over the competition. These need to be woven together with the compliance material that addresses the requirements of the RFP.
- Provide an environment for the team to have sufficient time for the front-end writing, as well as for necessary reviews, approvals, and especially for revisions that transform the initial ideas into a first-rate document. Develop a schedule; help the team maintain their pace; provide meetings for efficient brainstorming; and supply them with the best of your writing talent, facilitation skills, opinions, and enthusiasm.

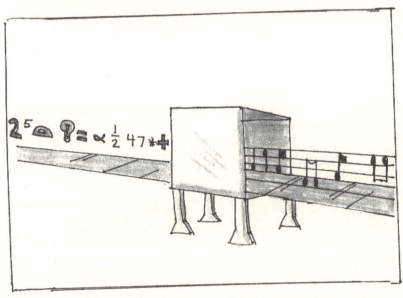

Once you're into full-stage writing of your proposal, we implore marketing staff to please take ownership. In many firms, marketing staff are still seen as mere support staff. Marketers increase their value when they show leadership skills and an ability to manage pursuits.

It takes only two seconds to understand that the economics of a technical professional services firm requires that it achieve its sales goals with minimal cost. Cost savings are derived when technical people invest the minimum amount of time required on non-revenue producing activities, while the firm employs as few overhead staff as possible. Firms must squeeze as much out of its business development program as it can, so technical and marketing staff must collaborate efficiently and wisely.

Accordingly, we believe that basic proposal organization and activities should be owned by marketing staff. They should organize the time of technical staff to meet the milestones and deadlines of the proposal document. However, in many organizations, marketers don't step up to the plate, or technical staff members feel they need to control the production process. This basic organizational challenge results in an immediate clash, resulting in an unprofitable business culture and unbalanced workload. Every high-performing team needs to marry the best skills of the team members to the tasks. Technical staff members that trust marketing professionals and marketing staff who earn that trust are the lifeblood of a healthy technical services business development program.

It is essential to obtain commitments for all resources. One sure way for a proposal to fall behind schedule is to assign people who are too busy with other priorities, or do not respect deadlines. During a major proposal effort, technical contributors must find a replacement for their day jobs as they slave away on the proposal. The reality is that your proposal will not stay on schedule if the key resources do not commit their time to complete assignments.

We also emphasize the importance of balancing completing the task, while allowing for creative inspiration. On one hand, a proposal leader deserves credit for cracking the whip and efficiently moving the team forward. On the other hand, you can be so focused on deadlines that you'll never develop the ideas that could make the difference between winning and losing. We concede that we've been in many proposal meetings that get sidetracked onto tangential technical discussions. But, marketers must remember that they're in a technical business, and a technical brainstorming session could be just what is needed to create a winning proposal. A good facilitator can effectively elicit great ideas from a technical meeting, while keeping the proposal on track.

Also, remember that technical genius comes in all shapes and sizes. While it would be easy for the marketer to spend time with the most polite and professional of technical staff, sometimes the best ideas originate from those who have the most disagreeable personalities. Equally, the most introverted of technical people, who are least likely to speak up during a noisy meeting, may also have brilliant ideas. It is up to the marketer's facilitation skills to draw out the best ideas.

The challenge of the marketer is to develop an environment in which all team members contribute at their highest value. The marketer who takes on more responsibility over the proposal process will be more successful in navigating rough waters. The successful marketer engages the right people for the right tasks, while assuring them that the proposal process is in good hands. That assurance comes from a track record of success and a work style that is organized, thoughtful, proactive, and energetic.

A calm, collected approach goes a long way to assuring your team that you have things well in hand. If you are prone to fits of drama, then you will give the impression of being out of control, inviting a manager to commandeer the proposal. In other words, display the desired behavior, and the results will follow.

We believe that the *servant leadership*[11] model is valuable to emulate. The Servant Leader is a

> *If you are assigned the leadership role for a proposal, why is your job one of the hardest in a technical professional services firm? Two reasons:*
> - *You need to recognize – and make peace with – the fact that proposals and sales are not the highest priority for technical professionals.*
> - *The busiest technical professionals have little spare time for precisely the same reason why you want them to work on the proposal— they're good at what they do.*
>
> *As a result, you will be challenged on two fronts: getting high quality content for your proposal, and getting it on time.*
>
> *But this doesn't mean there's no hope. The better firms have learned to improve their approach to proposals, along with training their technical professionals to place a higher priority on proposals. These firms have learned to start early, and finish early, and secure commitments from technical professionals to make strong contributions.*
>
> *In many cases, these firms decide not to submit as many proposals as other firms. Being more selective buys you more time from those technical professionals who are badly needed on only the most promising efforts.*

---

[11] Greenleaf, Robert K. *Servant Leadership: A Journey into the Nature of Legitimate Power and Greatness.* New York: Paulist, 1977.

finely tuned mix of tactician, worker-bee, and chameleon who can integrate with any group, employ hands-on skills, and create change from within.

The servant leader knows how to balance the need for technical staff to talk their way through the proposal. They have to circle it, sniff it, toss it around, toy with it, and complain about it, before they will be open to discussing what is important—how are you going to win? A good facilitator can guide the conversation toward fruitful decisions, but they have to let the team work it out. Since time is usually a critical factor, you must balance keeping an eye on the clock and moving the conversation forward.

Keep the Technical Team on Track

Staying on track during a proposal is a key element of efficiency and effectiveness. A good proposal kick-off meeting will set the stage, and allow the technical people who have competing priorities to get their heads into the proposal. The challenge is to balance the need for efficiency with the need to develop solutions and sales messages on a tight schedule. Those things, like any creative process, can only be achieved through conversation and messy brainstorming of ideas.

We've learned that a productive initial proposal meeting needs to harness the energy of the team and get them moving toward persuading the client to select your team. You've hopefully spent weeks, if not

> *When I was a young marketing coordinator, I worked many nights and weekends. My colleagues and I were corks on the sea, completely at the mercy of the deadlines that crashed over us. It was as if there was no past (because I blocked out memories of stressful proposals we had completed) and no future (because we were continuously focused on the deadlines of the present).*
>
> *When I became the marketing manager, I soon realized that I was not working as many late nights or over weekends.*
>
> *We were getting started earlier by being more proactive and setting deadlines. I made goals of getting proposals completed before holidays, convincing technical teams to meet internal deadlines. It's challenging to convince a project manager to finish a proposal a week before it's due (think of all the ideas they could develop in a whole week). But completing a project ahead of schedule and under budget is a worthy goal, for a project or a proposal.*
>
> *Good management means being in control of your destiny. When I became a manager of my world, my life changed.*

months, in positioning for the pursuit, and now with the RFP in hand, it's high time to raise two topics:

- <u>Assess the Client's Needs</u>. How does the project directly affect the client's business? Projects are rarely isolated. Knowing how it fits into the client's world is critical in placing the project in context of the client's mission. Being able to address that point is key to becoming trusted by your client.
- <u>Develop a list of direct benefits that the client will realize if they select you over the competition</u>. Differentiation is everything. Technical solutions can be provided by anybody, but the technical solutions that YOU provide in your own specific way give the client clear reasons to select you over everyone else. Also keep in mind that the benefits must be readily identifiable by the client in terms they understand. It is often a struggle to get technical staff to translate benefits they see in highly technical terms, to results of interest to clients.

At its most basic, your goal is to understand the client's challenges, then satisfy their needs. Since the client's organization may be represented by a number of people, understanding what drives them can be a complex undertaking. Keeping the focus of your technical people on the two items listed above will force the team to provide useful content for the proposal, instead of technical material that doesn't matter to the decision-makers.

Another valuable way to frame the conversations necessary for developing a winning proposal is to perform a SWOT analysis. Exploring Strengths, Weaknesses, Opportunities, and Threats is never a wasted exercise. The concept has been described in many other writings; there is not much that we can add to the process, except to advise you not to spend too much time analyzing the competition. We think too much investment is made in worrying about them. Certainly, you want to understand how to counteract their perceived strengths, but most of the time you're guessing. Worry about your relationship with the client, your understanding of their needs, and how to clearly communicate your ideas to them.

Respond to the client's request

We strongly recommend that a proposal checklist or compliance matrix be prepared as one of the first documents for guiding proposal preparation. A marketing coordinator should develop the list by reading every word of the RFP, and identifying every element requested by the client. Progress on the proposal checklist then becomes one of the main agenda items during status meetings.

Sometimes, clients dictate the order of sections within proposals, and at other times the respondent can decide. Either way, the checklist should be organized by section, with clear denotation of subsections that track with RFP requirements.

The proposal checklist can also define the appropriate reviews and approvals needed along the way. At a minimum, you should plan on what is commonly known as a Red Team[12] review for all but the simplest of proposals. The Red Team is an independent body of people to review submittals for compliance, quality, and verification that the team's message is properly conveyed. The team should be composed of individuals who know the subject matter, and are capable of thinking like a client. This point is not trivial – adding technical professionals to a Red Team who are incapable of understanding the point of view of a client will be of no help. Very helpful people are those who have been clients during their careers. For large proposals, you could certainly reach outside the firm for retired clients who may still want to work, in return for a stipend.

> For the largest and most strategic submittals, consider the value of a full range of review opportunities:
> - **Purple Team:** GO/NO GO decision. Looks for alignment with company strategic and tactical goals, including risk profile.
> - **Black Team:** Predict competitor response and/or solutions.
> - **Pink Team**: Confirms solution, and validates competitive strategy.
> - **Green Team:** Reviews cost/price of solution.
> - **Red Team:** Final proposal draft review, scores proposal against criteria as if they were client.
> - **Gold Team:** Final approval of proposal, including price.
> - **White Team:** Debrief, lessons learned from capture plan to proposal development and contract award.

Be sure to allow time in your schedule for responding to the Red Team (or other) review. There's no sense in investing the time and ex-

---

[12] The color review concept was developed by Federal agencies, we think. The color-scheme application to teams reviewing proposals has been greatly expanded to a spectrum of colors relating to commercial terms, pricing, competitors, and even lessons-learned. Origin is believed to be the US Army, but is difficult to pin-point.

pense of a review, then not having time to respond to the reviewer's comments. There are infinite levels of review possibilities—all of the colors of the rainbow.

Securing signatures goes hand-in-hand with reviews and approvals. Many firms have rules for signature authority; as a marketer you do not want to break these rules. Limits often include the dollar value of the proposed work, and the risk profile of the assignment. These approvals should be incorporated into the proposal schedule, along with checking to ensure that the right persons will be around to ink their signatures, when needed. If a proposal will require a highly placed executive or others for signature, then be sure to schedule a briefing for them in advance. You don't want to be running to the overnight courier office, and find yourself unable to answer all of the bosses' questions on the way. In some cases, electronic signatures are allowed by the client, whereas others require originals. Also, be sure to obtain permission before using an electronic signature.

Finish Early

We can't tell you how many nights, weekends, and holidays we've spent working on proposals. We can even attest to proofreading proposals on Christmas day. Why do proposal deadlines always come down to the last minute? We're convinced than many clients like to come back from a holiday to a desk load of proposals. Some also are interested in weeding out the consultants who aren't willing to sacrifice their vacation. But more often than not, poor time management on the part of marketers and technical professionals is the root of the problem. The difference between working to your own deadlines versus working to those dictated by the RFP is the difference between skiing down a mountain and falling down a mountain—being in control or out of control.

Completing a proposal on your own schedule means getting started early. The amount of time from the release of an RFP to its due date is always shorter than you need. **So, waiting to begin your proposal writing until you receive the RFP makes no sense.** If you want to worry about your competition, then worry about how large a jump they have on you. If they have strategically teamed with a prized partner six months prior to the RFP release, you should have gotten to that partner eight months prior. If your competition is meeting with the team to develop winning strategies ten months prior, you should be meeting twelve months prior. There's no better feeling than knowing you've done more than any of your competitors to secure a contract. And it's obvious to the client who's ahead of the game.

Develop a day-by-day schedule, running through the proposal due date, to the interview date, if known. Add float to the schedule, by working in a cushion of time before internal proposal milestones to allow for unforeseen delays. A team that uses its time efficiently can perform better than their confused and disorganized competition.

Can you spend too much time preparing a proposal? Certainly. One of the greater challenges in the proposal process is to know when enough is enough. If one of the strategies to winning a project is to get started early, another important decision is to know how much effort to invest.

> *Early in my career I relished the periods of ultra-emotional deadline-madness—that feeling of instability during challenging proposal preps. There was a lot of cussing, paper wadding, sleeve-rolling. Everyone else seemed to act that way; I thought it was how you got attention from the boss. They certainly seemed concerned for my wellbeing, but (I realized) not in a good way. They were worried that they might miss a deadline, I realized.*
>
> *I'm embarrassed to think back on it. It wasn't helpful to the process and exhibited a lack of control, the last thing for which I wanted to be known.*
>
> *Eventually, I found it to be more valuable to be a calming influence during stressful times. I became more proud of a reputation for stability, rather than tension.*
>
> *Every member of a team looks toward the marketer as a barometer of the pursuit. Is it going well or in danger of imploding? Even though many marketers have little control over whether a pursuit is ultimately won, the things they do have control over should be under control.*

A million dollar contract is a great accomplishment, but if it cost the firm $200,000 to achieve the win, you've spent all your potential profit before you even begin. Note that we may sometimes spend the profit on the pursuit of a job because there is more at stake with the client than a first assignment. A winning proposal can put you in the driver's seat for a long-term relationship. These are business decisions which should be thoroughly considered.

Another challenging decision-point in a pursuit is when you have identified a project early, invested significant effort in developing a proposal, and then the RFP is delayed. Proposal teams often continue to refine and rewrite, without thinking of the significant costs involved. As stated earlier, a profitable professional services business maximizes sales and minimizes costs. However, asking a business developer to minimize costs flies against their natural instinct to outgun the competition. If you could spend another month on the proposal, why wouldn't you? One solution is to know the client well enough to understand their selection process. Do they select on the basis of a proposal? Do they shortlist the most credible firms, then request interviews? If the latter, and if you have early indications that they find your team credible, then it makes no sense to develop a proposal worthy of Tolstoy. Rather, write one that's good enough to get shortlisted, finish early, turn the proposal over to the client, then invest most of your effort on preparing a killer presentation.

We understand that in the heat of battle, it's difficult to gauge how much effort is adequate to get to the next step of the procurement process. Understandably, no one wants to leave anything on the table, but certainly it's your responsibility to invest the company's money prudently. Our philosophy is to get the document done early.

A special note about pricing. Getting the right price into your proposal may be more important than all of your nicely written, formatted

> *There is an episode from the original Star Trek series that recounts a story about Captain Kirk as a cadet in Star Fleet Academy, participating in a final test before graduation. The young cadets are asked to captain a simulated starship in a disastrous war game scenario. The starship is facing the Klingons, who are bearing down for a final blow. It became called the Kobayashi Maru. This is the ultimate no-win situation. The intent is to see how each cadet faces imminent death.*
>
> *The story of how Captain Kirk faced this no-win situation had become legend. Captain Kirk changed the rules by sneaking into the facility before his final exam and re-programming the computer—allowing him to escape from the enemy.*
>
> *The lesson from repeated viewings of this episode (see, mom and dad, we did learn something from watching TV) is, "when faced with a situation in which you cannot be successful, change the rules."*
>
> *So what does one do in the technical services version of this quandary? If the competition is the incumbent, for example, convince the client of the need for a "fresh" perspective. If your rivals have more experience, provide the client with detailed drawings to prove your own skills. Whatever the weakness, point to a strength—and change the rules of engagement.*

text and graphics. Many RFPs stipulate that you provide price breakdowns showing detail for labor, expenses, overhead and profit. Moreover, they often want to see background information broken down by task or activity. For large projects where the cost is high, getting the price right and showing all of that detail can be a major challenge, and can take on a life of its own for the proposal team. It can be easy to make a mistake, as spreadsheets are manipulated in the heat of battle. We recommend that every line and column of every spreadsheet be checked by hand. There are no shortcuts, if you're going to assure accuracy for the most important part of a proposal.

Leave Nothing to Chance: Editing, Production and Delivery

The one essential skill for a marketer is to write with clarity. If a marketer or business developer can't write, they aren't providing much value to their firm. If they can't provide clarity of meaning or sales messages to a proposal, then all they're providing is formatting of someone else's ideas. The key to a marketer's career is to speak and write intelligently about technical solutions that they may not initially understand, but can clearly connect how these ideas benefit clients.

A marketer who is a good editor can remove extraneous information, meet the page limit, tease out the sales propositions, and make it interesting, even for a client who is forced to read 15 submittals. One key to interesting writing is to compress the language. This means using the fewest number of words to convey the intended information. On the opposite side, most technical professionals work with "details." The service they provide typically involves breaking down a project into finer and finer granularity, until it becomes comprehensible and manageable. The only way humans have been able to perform something as unimaginable as traveling to the moon has been through breaking the endeavor into thousands of individual, manageable tasks. However, for proposals, which are persuasive arguments, the goal is not to accumulate detail, but rather to summarize those details into a few memorable ideas that resonate with your clients.

> *In the early 90's, wanting to keep pace with the quality of our competitors' proposals, our firm bought one of the first color printers. It used specially coated paper and colored cellophane on three cylinders. A short time later, I was*

working on a particularly large document. I decided to use three-ring binders, because of the size of the document. After we reproduced the sets, we used a drill press to bore holes in the pages for the three-ring binding. By the sixth stack of paper, the drill bit was getting quite hot. Suddenly, we began to smell an odor that you never want to encounter during production of your proposal: Smoke!

Smoke equals fire; my proposal was on fire. The hot drill bit had ignited the chemical coating on the color pages. Well, the proposals arrived on time to the client, but they were a little charred around the binding and smelled a little smoky.

For every proposal, there's a story. That's what makes them memorable and the life of a marketer an adventure. You learn from every one.

Chapter 8
Winning Presentations and Interviews

Everything becomes a little different as soon as it is spoken out loud.
- Hermann Hesse, Author

You've just invested the better part of a year positioning and submitting a proposal for a major project. The client calls. "Congratulations, you've been shortlisted. You and three of your competitors are requested to tell us why we should select you?"

Your stomach drops. You were hoping the client would select you based on the brilliantly crafted proposal you wrote, or on the bid you painstakingly prepared. It's all on paper, you think. What more could they possibly need? They want me to take my masterpiece of written persuasion and my sharp-penciled bid list and turn them into a staged, theatrical drama?

So, you gather the technical team. You look around the table. None of your staff look like Meryl Streep, and you don't feel like William Shakespeare. You wonder, "What am I really supposed to do here?"

One of the more interesting rituals of the technical services procurement process, especially for engineers and architects, is the multistep approach of submitting a proposal, then participating in a presentation and interview in front of the client. This process of issuing an RFP, shortlisting, then requesting interviews has developed over many years as a preferred method to select a consultant, especially for public entities. The investment in time for both the client and the consultant is considerable. But because clients are buying skills and knowledge, rather than a product, it is understandable that they would like to meet and interview the people they are purchasing.

Unfortunately, many of the industry's most skilled professionals do not have an aptitude for public speaking. Yet, they often must carry the burden of convincing the client of their team's qualifications. A skilled speechmaker or salesperson cannot substitute for them, as clients demand to hear from the proposed technical team. So, the interview process has become one of the more challenging aspects of marketing in this industry—to guide technical staff to present their ideas in a way that connects emotionally and persuasively to an audience. Essentially, you're requiring your team to put on a high school play. Yes, there will be a script. Yes, we will talking about where to stand. Yes, we will tell you to speak louder and with more conviction. Yes, we will ask you to practice, practice, practice.

You can identify those people who were interested in drama in school, before their talents led them to technical services. And you can point out those people who naturally enjoy talking to large groups of other people. Some staff members relish these opportunities. They're worth their weight in million dollar contracts. Because, in the end, most large competitive contracts are won during the period of persuading clients individually prior to the RFP, then closing the deal with them collectively at the interview. It's all about standing up and saying, "This is why you should select us."

For most marketers and business developers, this is the sweet spot of sales. There's no better day at the office than one in which you pack the car with a laptop and a projector, load your smartest people in the back, drive to your client's office, and show them what your firm can do. Even sweeter is the moment of truth that occurs at a sales interview because of the direct intersection of technical people skilled in rocket science under the umbrella of performing arts.

Wait: a Word that Should be Banned from the English Language

Wait. As in, "Let's wait until we know more about the project. Let's wait until after we prepare our proposal. Let's wait for the shortlist to come out. Let's wait until we find out the interview date." There are a million reasons to wait before you start preparing for an interview with a client. Even teams that know for certain that an interview will be scheduled often wait until the last minute to prepare.

The reason is understandable. For technical professionals, developing a technical proposal is straightforward. It involves developing a bid, a scope of work, or an approach to a project. It involves wrestling technology or rocket science to the ground – great fun! But the task of creating a persuasive presentation, complete with communicating your commitment to a client, can be like asking a fish to bark like a dog. So, procrastination is a common problem to deal with because grappling with the art of human emotion is uncomfortable.

Developing a presentation can be a time-consuming process. From brainstorming messages to drawing charts and graphs to practicing your delivery, an interview can take a month or more to pull together. So, waiting for the client to put your presentation on the calendar is a serious mistake, but one which happens all the time.

Doing last things first

Most books on marketing technical services emphasize the importance of developing your presentation prior to your proposal, though the proposal is typically required by the client first. Developing the presentation's messages and proofs early in the pursuit is valuable for positioning with the client. They provide talking points for every meeting. The presentation, by its very nature, is also a useful outline for your proposal. You can weave those messages into the proposal, the cover letter, project descriptions, and resumes.

But there's no more challenging task than to ask your team to develop the last element first. It requires willpower that we often don't possess. But it's also a leadership opportunity for marketing and business development staff members. A marketer who can rally their team to proactively work in this non-linear fashion can be the most important person in the sales process.

So what does it mean to start your pursuit with the presentation? Simply this: ask and answer a few simple questions (from the point-of-view of the client) before you get too far down the road. These questions should be built into your Go/No Go decision, as you will likely not win the project if you can't answer them convincingly:

1. What are three reasons why we should select you, rather than your competitors?
2. What are the three greatest challenges to the success of this project and how do you propose to engage with each one?
3. Who is the leader of your team? What has he/she accomplished that would benefit me and my organization?
4. Where have you successfully completed a similar project that faced similar challenges?

If you and your team can't persuade a non-technical, independent observer (your mother, perhaps) with your answers to these questions, then there's no reason you should spend precious business development dollars on the pursuit.

Hint: the following answers are NOT persuasive:

- We are available.
- We are local.
- We are excited.
- We would really like to do this interesting project (because we've never done one before).
- Our team leader is qualified— you haven't met him, but trust us, he's really good.
- We're the best at this type of project (often stated breezily without proof).

Step one of any pursuit is to answer these questions, then tell your client at every available opportunity. The process for answering these questions is the definition of "capture planning." And the process for bouncing your responses and ideas off the client, then refining them, based on their feedback, is "positioning." So, if you've prepared the answer to these questions, you've developed much of what will most likely be required in a proposal and at an interview.

Most importantly, this advanced preparation can shave several days off of the time needed to prepare the interview. There is never enough time between the shortlist and the interview! That valuable time can be spent rehearsing, rather than developing and endlessly refining content.

You may want to ask us, "How many presentations were wasted efforts because you proactively developed them, but then did not get shortlisted?" Our answer is, "a few, and we're proud of it." We wear them like badges of honor, because they are examples of doing everything right. And everyone knows that often you do everything right and are still not selected. Nearly none of our interview efforts have been a waste. If you do the right things early, you receive rewards later.

So, as a marketer, your job is to swim against the current, upstream of the shortlist announcement, and get your team ready for the interview before they think they need to. Let's talk about some nuts and bolts.

- Everyone uses Power Point.
- Foam core boards are used sometimes, but they are most often requested by internal staff remembering the good old days.
- Limit your presentation to one slide for every 1 ½ minutes of allotted time. So, for 30 minutes, use no more than 20 slides. Seriously.
- Handouts are a good thing, if for no other reason than they focus the presentation team on the main messages. They can also be helpful for incorporating content which was left out of the proposal, or raised by the client after reading the proposals. These should not be developed as an after-thought, half-way through rehearsals when someone says, "Hey, are we doing a handout?" You should plan on having a hardcopy handout in the event of a power failure.
- Do not give the client the handout before the presentation. The minute you hand it to them, and throughout your presentation, they will flip through it instead of listening to you.

What does a great presentation look like?

A great presentation is simple and clear; it is an artfully choreographed ballet of speakers, each with a memorable and convincing message that differentiates your team from anyone else the client is considering. It uses visuals as an "aid" to reinforce the message. It has no extraneous elements and zero slides that are hard to read.

One of the most important jobs for the marketer during the process of developing a great presentation is to create complementary and convincing visual aids. Power Point slides, boards, flip charts, videos—whatever it is, they need to complement the message, be understandable in mere moments by the audience, and not be distracting.

We could write an entire chapter on the visual component of technical presentations. In fact, there are many templates, guides, and other tools that help the marketer develop compelling graphics. But we think marketers and technical teams tend to obsess over the slides. Interview teams spend an inordinate amount of time talking about colors, fonts, and animation on their slides. Important, for sure, but keep your focus on what sells—your people talking to clients. Too often, the visual component is either a barrier between your staff and the client, or a crutch to avoid developing and delivering winning messages. FOCUS ON THE CONTENT, NOT THE MEDIA.

So, let's get quickly past the slide show itself:
- They are not the speaker's notes; they're visual complements to the topic under discussion. If we had a dollar for every slide we've seen that sported hundreds of words, we'd be sitting on the beach in Hawaii, instead of working. Rule of thumb: 5 bullets, 5 words in each bullet maximum. We pride ourselves on our bullet-less presentations, using only graphic illustrations. It's incredibly refreshing.

- Simplify the look and feel. Many marketers who double as graphic designers often clutter presentations with overlays, headers, and other design elements. Keep slides simple and clean.
- When animation was first introduced in graphic software, everyone jumped all over it. Now, it is passé. Just move from one to the next. Sure, video can be effective, but bullets flying across the screen are distracting. Also, fussing with animation adds preparation time, and can distract the presentation team from the content.
- If you're a technical staff member, project manager, or corporate vice president— your expertise is not in choosing the color of the background on the slides. Focus instead on the messages and on your powers of persuasion.

The role of the coach

The marketer who coaches the interview team has a critical role. First, technical leaders have too much on their plates to manage the many details that are part of a presentation. The marketer should be responsible for everything related to assuring that the event comes off without a hitch. (The number of lost power cords, broken easels, and projector failures is an indication that many presentations require someone skilled in event planning.)

In addition, because this is a "performance," a coach is needed to act as an audience to assure that the messages are being communicated effectively. No one who is part of the presentation is able to view it objectively, in the same way you would not ask an actor to review their own performance. A coach helps refine the presentation as it is being developed. The iterative process of creating a presentation is much more fluid and active than a proposal. A tweak here or there, shaving a minute from one person's presentation, can change the entire tone of the interview. An experienced coach, like a theater director, can meld individual speeches into an integrated performance.

A question we are asked by marketers is, "How do you learn to coach an interview?" The answer, of course, is to watch and learn. It is easier to learn to develop proposals, as managers and marketers are working side-by-side. But in an interview, senior managers often take over and the junior staff members are left outside of the room. The only way junior technical and marketing people can learn the craft of coaching an interview is to sit and watch. So, advice to all junior staff: talk your boss into letting you stay in the room while the sausage is being made.

There is an art to being effective in the role of coach. It is never about yelling out, "Say it with feeling!" Heavy-handed direction (as in theater) can do more to stamp out a good technical presentation than draw it out. Especially with technical staff who are unfamiliar with being in front of clients (the PhD's, the specialists, the backroom geniuses). These people often win projects because of their expertise; they are crucial, yet need to be coaxed into communicating that expertise to non-technical selection committees.

Coaching the unskilled speaker

The job of the coach is to draw out the best performance from the team. One of the greatest challenges, therefore, is working with people who are not natural performers, who entered the profession thinking that public speaking would not be required of them.

The easiest way to avoid the challenge is not to use them. Many firms have "go-to" people they use for all presentations. (Not surprisingly, these people often appear prominently on proposal organization charts, but rarely show up on the project, when selected.) That approach can work, until it creates a chokepoint, limiting your ability to win new business when those people are overloaded. In addition, some pursuits require a technical specialist to speak on a complex subject that cannot be faked by anyone else. Sooner or later, most firms will be faced with putting an unskilled speaker in front of a client.

The unskilled speaker is challenged with learning the craft of public performance on-the-job. Though most firms have training programs, and many technical professionals participate in activities such as Toastmasters (highly recommended), real skills can only be gained through actual experience, sometimes during high-stakes, multi-million dollar pursuits. The coach's job is to teach them to pilot a plane, while in the air, carrying a planeload of passengers. The key to success, in our minds, is to focus on keeping the plane in the air, while making changes in small increments. Keeping both hands on the controls, moving knobs with small motions, is an art that a talented coach brings to the party. Some of the tools that an unskilled speaker and coach can employ include:
- <u>Writing a script and memorizing it.</u> Both the speaker and coach can collaborate to develop a presentation that can be refined

through extended rehearsals. However, this can be time-consuming and may result in a less natural performance. The better alternative is to develop notes, memorizing the key words, then eventually discarding the notes. It is best to perform this off-line. We often see a roomful of people trying to work with one speaker that needs to catch up. This can be inefficient and actually cause the speaker to lock-up in front of his/her peers, difficult from which to recover. Taking the person out of the room, practicing with them one-on-one, then re-introducing them into the collective, can work well.

- <u>Practicing the important use of body language.</u> A less than eloquent speaker can make up a lot of ground through effective body language. Eye contact is 75% of effective communication. Yet, this is an underused skill. The speaker and coach can work together to refine making eye contact with the audience, using hand gestures to provide emphasis, and walking around the room to maintain attention. This type of practice can build confidence in a nervous speaker.
- <u>Being realistic</u>. We often build a presentation, then populate the structure. It is important to be realistic about the skills of your staff and develop a presentation that uses their skills to your best advantage. It is probably not a good idea to assign your poorest speaker as the closer. Put your weakest speaker in the middle of the presentation, so that your strongest players open and close the show. Seems logical, but it means thinking about the structure of your presentation in a different way.

We recommend the coach be the singular source of guidance to the unskilled speaker. The rest of the presentation team, while meaning well, should refrain from adding their points of view. Nothing is more confusing than receiving direction from multiple, often conflicting, coaches.

Coaching the Uncoachable

Working with an unskilled speaker is a challenge, but there's a lot of satisfaction in watching someone's skills progress. The bigger obstacle to successful presentations is technical staff members who are uncoachable. These are the people who need skill-building, but who struggle to improve. They lock up and get worse as the practice sessions proceed. A large part of the coach's job is to identify the style of each speaker, then alter their coaching style to match the speaker's needs. The coach will be able to make larger changes in some people, smaller changes in others. It is not helpful to create a roomful of frazzled people, because the coach can't gauge the style of the members of the team.

And here's the tricky part: the way people speak in rehearsals can be completely different from the way they speak in an actual interview. Intense pressure does peculiar things to people. It is critical for a marketer to attend actual interviews to obtain a sense of the people he/she is working with. Many times, clients do not mind if a person from the team sits in the back of the room and watches. We've sat through dozens of interviews, watching how our teammates interact with clients during this important phase of the sales process. Our advice to marketers: get in the room!

> *War Story: The pursuit is a new transit system through downtown. Millions in consulting and design fees. I was a young marketing coordinator. We had vice presidents arrive from across the country to make the presentation. The client imposed a strict 30-minute time limit. The firm decided to use a new technology, laserdisc, with illustrations and animation of the proposed route of the new transit system.*
>
> *Well, the entire team became so entranced with the technology that we spent two weeks perfecting the show. Even on the last morning, they were tweaking words and pictures, before burning the presentation to a giant shiny disc. The problem was that they never took the time to rehearse the whole presentation. And the out-of-town vice-presidents never practiced once. We thought, "Gee, they must be good, if they don't need to rehearse." And who was I to tell a VP to practice?*
>
> *At the interview, they did a great job for 30 minutes. The technology impressed the client, you could tell. At the 30-minute mark, the client's alarm sounded. They said, "Time's up." WE WERE ONLY HALFWAY THROUGH THE PRESENTATION! "Thank you, have a good day," said the client. We were cooked. What I learned: I don't care if you're the President of China. You're rehearsing.*

Here are some of the differences that occur between the practice and the actual interview.

- Going long: Almost all interviews are time-limited. We often have to squeeze the interview and assign strict time controls on the team. Some people rehearse their section perfectly, hone it, but when they get into the actual interview, they lose their sense of time. That has sunk more interviews than we can count. We think the reason is, once a client is in the room, some people simply think up more things to say. Also, all that helpful coaching tends to cram extra ideas and sound-bites into the speaker's head, and they're screaming to be blurted out. **Solution**: Make your speakers aware of their tendencies. Self-awareness is an antidote to many bad habits.

- Going Commando: Some people just can't say the same thing the same way twice. They take a look at the selection committee and then make a snap judgment that the topic they practiced is not right for the situation. They speak to an entirely different topic. Good sales people can think on their feet and are flexible, but in a team interview setting, their change in direction sometimes leaves everyone else in the dust. **Solution**: Continually remind players of their role as part of a team. They certainly should understand that consistency is important on their projects; why not in interviews?
- Mixed Messages: Pursuit champions often build an organization chart without thinking about the interview. Sometimes a Project Manager with a strong personality is most useful as a technical advisor. Likewise, sometimes a timid junior staff member will be a perfect (or most available) manager for a project. However, in an interview, attempting to build up a meek manager, while toning down a strong advisor, can be a real challenge. We've faced many situations in which a person in a minor role on the org chart overpowers a mild project manager, causing confusion about who's in charge of the project. The real challenge is during Questions and Answers, when natural instincts take over, a good reason for the coach to attend and take mental notes. **Solution**: It takes strong facilitation skills, and a trusting team. The coach has to sort it out during the practice sessions, and has to be able to tell very senior staff members to shut up.
- Locking up: Some people have no problem speaking in front of their fellow employees. But when they get in front of clients, their nerves take over. Stage fright is a problem that is not always solved through experience. We know people in their fifties who still struggle with shyness. It's an understandable part of someone's personality. Keep this in mind when building the capture plan for your pursuit. Too often, we see people placed at the head of a multi-million dollar pursuit who cannot close the deal at the

interview stage. The answer to this problem can be to place the capable, but shy staff member as an assistant to the project manager, excusing them from heavy-hitting at the interview, yet keeping them in a prominent place on the team. **Solution**: Private one-on-one coaching time is an important tool to build a speaker's confidence.

Other Coaching Tips
- The coach sets the tone for the practice sessions. Like a play Director, the coach's job is to build up a confident team of performers. It is important to manage discussion during rehearsals. Egos can be destroyed with insensitive commentary. Also, mental overload can occur even in the most seasoned presenter Overwhelmingly detailed comments from the team can result in "lock-up" or a focus on details that lose sight of the important messages the team needs to deliver.
- There's also a tendency for everyone in the room to provide "helpful" comments. The coach should be the only person talking to the cast, especially as the number of rehearsals increase. Anyone with something urgent to say should relay it through the rehearsal

> *Two recent trends in client interviews are worth noting:*
> - *Interviews with no formal presentation. Instead, the interview consists entirely of responding to questions.*
> - *Interviews where the team is asked to make a presentation based on a topic or set of topics which are not revealed until you arrive for the interview. Your team will have a set period of time to prepare.*
>
> *Many technical professionals will respond to these trends by throwing up their hands and contending there is no point to rehearsing.*
>
> *For both situations, you should still attempt to anticipate a majority of the questions asked by the client, and rehearse your responses. Also, for the situation where you'll be required to prepare a presentation on the spot, you can rehearse this in advance, as well. Time and energy must be invested in brainstorming potential topics to be asked by client, and actually preparing charts and graphics.*
>
> *As a marketer, you'll be challenged to focus the team. Their tendency will be to spend less time because of the uncertain nature of the assignment, and you must exhort them to spend more time.*

manager, who will then decide whether something needs to be said. This is especially a challenge when company big-shots are invited to the interview.
- Ad-libbing is good to a point, then it drops off precipitously as you create "cognitive dissonance" with the audience. Ad-libs tend to grow with each rehearsal as ideas are raised and then stuffed into the presenter's head.

Questions and Answers

Many presentations are structured to allow a formal presentation by the technical professional team, followed by a period of questions and answers. Many teams focus on the element they can most control—the interview. Our experience tells us that most selection committees make their ultimate decision based on the performance during the Q&A period. Presentation teams, in our opinion, need to invest as much time practicing Q&A as they invest in practicing the interview. That rarely happens, though.

A basic strategy to prepare for Questions and Answers is to develop a list of questions you anticipate the selection committee might ask, then prepare answers for them. In our experience, a well-positioned team can anticipate as many as 80% of the questions. This is a real test of the quality of the team's positioning. Do they really know the client? If they say, "I have no idea what's on their mind." They should be in the client's office the next day finding out.

A good coach brings a list of questions that have been asked in previous interviews with that particular client. It is a good starting point for brainstorming, as many clients have similar concerns, "What does your team intend to do for us? Where have you done it before?" There are many obvious questions for which your team should prepare.

The Q&A period is not only a place for your client to clarify what they heard in the presentation, it is also a test of your team's organizational skills and ability to work together. The obvious focal point is the project manager. Clients are looking for signs that the PM is able to manage his/her team. One such sign is managing the pressure-filled interview period.

The project manager should be seen as the leader of the team the moment they walk into the room. They should lead the most important elements of the presentation, and certainly should direct the responses to the client's questions during Q&A. This is not to say that they should answer every question, but they should facilitate the responses. The client should know instantly to whom to direct a question. The project manager should consider the question, gain any needed clarification, then decide how best to respond.

Again, success in this area leads back to the critical decisions made week, months, sometimes a year earlier. Who you select to be project manager will eventually lead to that person being in a roomful of people, guiding the team through responses to complex questions. How well you've chosen your project support team will be revealed in this short period of time. Yet, we often see these decisions made casually, based on either availability or technical skills. A winning project team is a group of smart people who work well together, who can anticipate questions, understand the political context of a situation, and tell the client what they need to know.

> *If you were to graph the percentage of time a typical team spends preparing the interview, it would look something like this:*
> - *Practicing Q&A = 10%*
> - *Practicing interview = 30%*
> - *Tweaking the slides = 60%*
>
> *The interview coach should strive for the following percentages:*
> - *Practicing Q&A = 40%*
> - *Practicing interview = 40%*
> - *Tweaking the slides = 20%*
>
> *The visuals are important, but are a smaller element than the practiced performance of the team. And the team should practice the Q&A for a length of time equal to the interview rehearsals.*

We've been in situations where the project manager answered every question, while his high-paid team of experts sat on their hands. We've seen Q&A periods in which the project manager never said a word, passively and happily watching everyone else. This is where a coach earns their pay, to strike the right balance and tone for this part of the "performance." Clients are closely watching this interaction between the members of the team, and are making up their mind right there (usually not while they read your beautiful proposal, or listen to your rehearsed presentation). The Q&A is ground zero for decision-making.

Answers to questions should be thoughtful and concise. Team members, after being called upon by the project manager, should pause briefly to collect their thoughts, and answer questions in a clear and compact manner. One of the best ways to answer questions is "Yes, but... or "No, because... or in the form of: "First..., second..., and third..." These are ways to verbally organize your response, so that the client can clearly follow your line of reasoning.

Benefits need to be explicitly stated. Technical people make this mistake all the time. They are fond of touting benefits which are recognizable only by peers in their profession. Many selection committees are made of non-technical people. Benefits should be based on the concept of proving the clients with solutions that are cheaper, better, faster (as we described in our chapter on Competitive Strategies).

Someone in the interview team should be responsible for writing down the questions. This helps the responder with multi-part questions. Under the pressure of an interview, there is a tendency to respond to the last part of a multi-part question, forgetting the beginning. It is critical (we know it's obvious, but we've seen the opposite) to answer the entire question. In addition, a list of questions can be returned to the marketer, who should keep a stockpile of questions for future interview practice sessions.

Scenarios and Solutions For the Q&A Period

As with the formal presentation itself, we've seen plenty of mistakes made during Q&A. Here are some common scenarios and recommended approaches.

- **Piling on.** Hard to resist, but it happens all the time. Everyone at an interview wants a chance to contribute, which is natural. A well-conceived presentation provides a showcase to all who are in attendance. However, some people feel the need to shine during every question asked of the team. This leads to a tendency for everyone to attempt to add their perspective to every answer. The results dilute the message, confusing the client, and wasting precious time. The more you talk without a script, the less convincing the response becomes. **Solution:** Interviews are practiced; Q&A needs to be equally practiced, and "rules of engagement" need to be developed and adhered to. Rules should include the maximum amount of time and speakers to be devoted to each response. Perhaps something like: no more than two speakers after the initial response for a maximum of one minute.

- **Mr. Can't-Stop-Talking**. Related to the above, the pressure of an interview setting often brings some people's latent personality traits to the forefront. One of the most common pratfalls during Q&A is the person who won't shut up. In an everyday setting, these people tend to be talkative, but in the most extreme, they literally try to answer every question posed by the client, regardless of whether or not they know the topic. In some cases, they interrupt other members of the team. **Solution**: a good coach can stop them before they do damage, brief them on the ground rules, or in the worst of conditions, leave them at home.

- **Presenters who aren't employees**. Subconsultants or other outsiders on your team may be your biggest risk. They can be unpredictable. You do not work with them every day, so you do not know what they may say or do. Also, there is a tendency to be more polite with outsiders than you would be with your own staff, and so directness is avoided. **Solution**: one way to minimize the risk is to spend time with them, and to be clear about your rules for presentations.
- **Arguing in front of the client**. Don't laugh, this happens. Presentation teams, especially if you have outside subconsultants, sometimes disagree with each other. The intent of the rehearsal period is to get everyone on the same page. However, during

Q&A, the team may be presented with a topic for which they have not prepared. **Solution**: It's better to let one person answer, than for different opinions to emerge from among the team. The coach needs to watch carefully for any signs of disagreement and assure that issues are completely vetted in the privacy of the rehearsal room.

- **Control is Absolute**. A bright technical person who speaks without thinking could lose an opportunity for you in ten seconds. Weeks, if not years of preparation and investment could go down the drain quickly. **Solution**: the coach needs to be empowered to not bring certain individuals to the presentation, no matter how technically qualified or how high up in management they may be.

Interview Order: First or Last?

In the same way that pilots continually talk about the mystery of Amelia Earhart, marketers are obsessed with interview order. If you have a choice, is it more advantageous to make your presentation first? You can set the bar, set minefields for your competitors, and not have to respond to questions set-up by competitors who preceded you. Or is it best to be the last presenter? You can be the final exclamation point in front of your client, the last people they see before they make their decision.

There's no question, the worst spot is being in the middle, right after lunch. Sleepy clients are your worst nightmare (we often bring caffeinated cola and candy for clients, when we're stuck in this time slot).

After a combined 50 years of business development and marketing experience, we have arrived at the perfect algorithm for selecting the best timeslot, when given a choice.

- If 4 or more interviews are scheduled in a single day, select 3rd (by the 4th interview, the clients are brain dead).
- If fewer than 4 in a day, select last.
- If interviews are spread over 2 or more days, pick last, or any available slot on the last day.
- If you have a solution that questions the validity of the incumbent's previous work on the project, request to be first (to assure presenting before the incumbent).

Most often, you have no choice, and are given a timeslot of the client's choosing. But it's still enjoyable to calculate the benefits of positioning.

Presentation Skills Training

Practicing presentation skills is important training for any technical professional. Every firm should place this training at the top of their list for employees you intend to participate in interviews. Training of this type usually involves gathering people into teams, then giving them a fictional project for which they prepare and present an interview. Practicing the skills discussed in this chapter, in a no-pressure setting, is a good way for people to improve their ability to win competitive work.

One valuable activity in which an interview team, marketer, or coach can participate is "acting" as the client during an interview practice at a presentation skills class. Being in your client's head, watching several teams make presentations on the same subject is eye-opening. You see several things when you're in this situation that you don't see when you are working only as part of a presentation team.

1. You see the similarity of teams. Everyone seems to come up with similar solutions to age-old problems. This makes it doubly important to ruthlessly develop unique benefits that only ONE team can provide, making it a slam dunk for the client to select you.
2. You see how little you can remember, after watching three, four, or five interviews in a single sitting. You quickly become numb after watching as few as three, 15 minute presentations. Unless you take incredible notes (which many clients do not), you can't remember who said what, especially if you do not know the presenters well.
3. You see the importance of true communication skills, especially eye contact. You make a connection with those people who speak to YOU, rather than to the screen.

By placing yourself in the client's shoes, you can view your future interviews in a whole new light. Here's how to respond to many of the challenges: Distill, distill, distill, and then distill some more. Technical people want to pack interviews with details, because it interests them. Focus on the interests of the selection committee, then clearly state your points (no more than three simple reasons the client should select you). Coaches have a continuous battle with technical staff over "educating the client." The emphasis on the technical aspects of a project at the interview phase is often a mistake. The client cannot possibly be educated during a one-hour interview, and they can't possibly retain all the technical detail of a multi-volume proposal. You are there to convince them to select you, not to teach them the intricacies of the project. The team needs to focus on the selling messages and compelling proofs, leaving the schematics at the door.

One of the most useful exercises, especially if the team is spinning its wheels or if the presentation is running too long (often the case), is to review the presentation one slide at a time, asking each presenter to capture the message on that slide in one sentence. Reinforcing a singular message will provide clarity to their presentation.

Finally, don't let speakers stand in front of the projector light; it shines words all over their face, and is annoying. And for goodness sake, don't use a laser pointer. You'll put someone's eye out with that thing.

> *You're frazzled, but still alive. The presentation team is at the client's office. After a week of arm-wrestling over slides, and arguing over questions and answers, you're left cleaning up the conference room. Suddenly the door bursts open; the team is back. You probe each member for their review of the presentation. Each is guardedly optimistic. You go over the questions asked by the client, and quiz the team on their responses.*
>
> *In a scary way, there were no glaring errors, only quiet confidence about each individual's contribution to a solid team effort. Someone remarks that all that time spent was worth it – they were ready for every question, and weren't caught off guard.*
>
> *Days go by. No word. Then the project manager takes a phone call, and word quickly spreads with the great news that your firm has been selected. He stops by your office and thanks you for everything, and you realize that the effort was worthwhile.*

Chapter 9
Closing the Deal

It ain't over 'til it's over.
- Yogi Berra, Professional Baseball Player,
Manager, and American Philosopher

A number of years ago, we were proposing to a large City for a program management assignment, and had not positioned as well as the competition. They had helped the City staff to create the opportunity, and were thought to have it wired. Our pursuit leader was one of my mentors. It seemed that he had half the company working on the proposal; those of us who were involved count it as a seminal learning experience.

For the interview, I played a minor technical role, but endured more rehearsals than I had ever experienced before, or since. Not surprisingly, the interview was one of the best ever, because each presenter peaked at the right time, despite some rough rehearsals. The question and answer period went even better; we had anticipated every single question and had prepared a response for most of them.

After the interview, we celebrated at lunch. Our team leader announced that phases one and two of the pursuit were now complete, and it was time for phase three. I was dumbfounded because I thought we were done, and that it would only be a matter of waiting for the outcome. Little did I know that our team would receive a unanimous vote from the selection committee, but that we might not be awarded the contract.

When is the selection committee decision final? In reality, the sale isn't complete until the contract is signed, notice to proceed is in your hand, and the client is prepared to process your invoice. Many marketers and business developers mistakenly assume their work is done once the last question is answered at an interview. We often wait for news, with bated breath, in anticipation of winning, then moving on to perform the work. For the simplest of cases, you may receive a phone call or letter with the good news, to be followed by contract negotiations. In reality, the passing of the interview as an event only marks the end of a phase in the selection process.

Imagine the confusion created in the mind of the rocket scientist, who has endured the rehearsal and delivery of the interview, and believes that the selection committee's choice is clear and simple—to choose the most elegant technical solution. We wish it were that simple, but unfortunately art often trumps science when human emotion governs choices.

After the Selection Process

As discussed in our chapter on decision-makers, selection committees do not always have the authority to make final decisions, much to the chagrin of technical professionals who assume the opposite. As a matter of fact, instances in which decisions have been modified or even overturned are not a rarity. Some selection committees may be acting only in an advisory role, with no formal authority. Often, management and/or an oversight organization reviews decisions, then makes the final award.

Although this seems like it should go without saying, how you deal with a win or loss is very important to future success. If you win, gloating to your competition is always a bad idea. The competitor you tease today may hold the keys to a teaming decision tomorrow. If you lose, never give the client a hard time. If there was ever a time to keep your emotions in check, it's after a loss. By even slightly questioning the decision, you could be burning a bridge for a long time. Satisfying your short-term feelings of disappointment could ruin in a matter of moments a relationship crafted by others in your firm over a long period of time.

> Let's overstate the obvious. Managers and decision-makers exist to, well, make decisions. While many technical people view their perfect solutions as the final answer, managers often regard technology as a "black box," only one of many factors in selecting you for the work. This is the entire point of our book. So, it's not surprising that technically dominated selection committee recommendations can be overturned by higher authorities only "doing their jobs."

If you lose, be aware that other events may put you back in the game. What if the selected firm is unable to negotiate a contract? Negotiations break down over cost or many other issues, such as terms and conditions. A great many selection processes contain established rules which dictate that if the client is unable to negotiate with the selected firm, then they move on to the next highest ranked firm. While this doesn't happen every day, it is not a rare occurrence – most marketers can readily cite examples of this happening during their careers. If you handle a loss with professionalism and dignity, you will reinforce the notion that you deserved to be placed so closely to the top. Your behavior during the days and weeks following a decision may do more to position your firm for the next opportunity than many other activities.

Protesting a Decision

We are frequently asked if a firm should ever protest an unfavorable decision. Many public agencies and private companies have formal procurement procedures and policies with provisions for protest. Over the years, the Federal government has also published fairly extensive protest rules. But does this mean you should do it, if you feel your firm has been wronged? Hardly.

Keep in mind that a protest essentially constitutes a formal questioning of the judgment of your client. We've never seen a client react well to this. Moreover, a protest can delay the final contract award while an investigation is conducted. We've seen these last up to a year. During this period of time, as your client's project falls increasingly behind schedule, who do you think will be blamed? Even if you had allies on the selection committee, the slow due-diligence of the investigation can turn even the best of friends against you. All of this means that you'll be laying your relationships on the line over not winning, risking future goodwill and future opportunities.

We also often hear that wrongdoing or other monkey business are valid reasons for protest. We have no quarrel with the basic point, but these are serious allegations which are difficult to prove. Technical professionals are often prone to accusations, especially in light of their reverence for technology, and inherent belief in their own superiority. Moreover, they believe that improprieties conducted by the competition are common rationalizations for losses. The conspiracy theorist believes in their presence when many times the competition has positioned better, has better relationships, formulated a better winning strategy, and just plain outfoxed them.

Except in certain situations, we recommend that cooler heads prevail and that the energy invested in a protest be redirected to a strong debrief, to learning from mistakes, and to building on strengths and overcoming weaknesses to position for the next opportunity. In the eyes of most people, handling defeat in a business-like manner will improve your chances for the next win by solidifying your reputation as a professional who can deal with adversity, with whom they want to do work.

Maintaining Contact with the Selection Committee after the Submittal or Interview

In our experience, we see many benefits in maintaining contact with the selection committee, especially if the decision is not taken immediately after the final interview. Sometimes, this may be difficult, or even potentially a violation of rules. If rules or policies exist, it is your responsibility to know and respect them. Adverse consequences can mean disqualification, or worse. However, if your firm is not forbidden from further contact, then a great deal can be done following the interview. Additional contact can allow you to hear about concerns regarding your team expressed by selection committee members. In some cases, you may be able to respond by furnishing more information, or make clarifications.

Your demeanor during this stage of the procurement can set up a positive (or negative) future relationship with the client. Remember that this is only one contract in perhaps a lifetime of future work opportunities. Not only are you trying to be selected for this single opportunity, but you're attempting to become a trusted, long-term partner with your client. By providing objective advice, clarification, or other support during the procurement process, you're previewing professionalism and friendship that will be valuable to them in the future.

Appealing to a Higher Authority

As a last resort, you should be prepared to deal with authority higher than the selection committee. This may include management or political decision-makers at multiple levels. But you should tread carefully. It is always delicate when you go over the head of peers at a client's organization. The old saying that it pays to have friends in high places applies when you have a big deal on the line. If you've done your homework, and have positioned well, then you have these relationships in place, so that you can approach them.

If you're selling to public agencies that are governed by politicians, all of the rules about getting to know the decision-makers still apply except that extra caution is advised. This is because politicians think differently from staff, and plainly speaking you can get in a lot of trouble by going over the heads of your friends. Any conflict created between levels of decision-making can spell doom for your firm. In our experience, many politicians expect to be approached, much to the discomfort of client management staff. This is because the vast majority of politicians expect to talk to a lot of people, especially firms selling to their organizations. They make a valid point in claiming to want to know more about the firms with whom they invest public money. In the best of all possible worlds, you should take your colleagues aside and inform them that you are making contact with political decision-makers without betraying their confidence.

Contract Negotiations

Finalizing and signing the contract is the last major area of involvement for marketers and business developers during procurement. In many firms, this responsibility is assigned to company officers who manage client relationships. But the marketing team has a role in supporting basic contract negotiations and reaching closure on the deal. To be sure, this is not a book on negotiating, nor do we offer legal advice on terms and conditions. But the behind-the-scenes work of the marketing team can be critical to success.

An oldie but goodie reference by Herb Cohen[13] succinctly summarizes the contract negotiation process.

> As an additional word to the wise, you should not necessarily feel compelled to get to know everyone in your client's upper management structure. First, this is probably not going to happen – if you're selling to a Fortune 500 company, don't expect to get any time with the CEO. To the extent possible, you should try to achieve some visibility with folks at this level, but don't spend an inordinate amount of time with those not involved in selecting technical professional services providers.

The author contends that the key elements of a negotiation are "infor-

---

[13] Cohen, Herb. You Can Negotiate Anything. Secaucus, NJ: L. Stuart, 1980.

mation, time, and power." Of these elements, the marketing team is unlikely to be able to impact time or power, but information should be in their wheel house. In general, the marketing team should take the lead in ensuring that homework is done for a range of topics, including:

Pricing

We like to see pricing discussions begun early, as with everything else, during capture planning. With experienced technical professionals, it doesn't take long to develop a "back of the envelope" estimate of your fee. Your estimate can be honed as time goes on, and as more understanding of the project is brought to the table. Moreover, talking price with the client early on is a worthwhile exchange.

Beware of racing through assembly of a price at the eleventh hour of proposal production. Quite often, this becomes a rushed activity with the deadline looming. This leaves the negotiation team at a disadvantage, defending numbers that were not thoughtfully developed. So, a helpful marketer should facilitate a time management strategy during the proposal process that allows estimators to develop quality pricing. Also, while this should go without saying, be cautious to avoid math errors. Quality assurance procedures apply to all marketing documents. We recommend hand-checking numbers.

One of the greatest challenges in producing a large proposal is to establish consistency between the "big three:" (1) scope of work, (2) level of effort, and (3) price. Most firms have standard spreadsheets, but the marketer may find him/herself in a three-way dance of changing data. In addition to maintaining consistency, documenting "assumptions" will add enormous value to the proposal, as the negotiating team advances its cause. For large proposals, you should name a "commercial manager" to be in charge. This person gathers the team responsible for assembling the scope, level of effort, and price while undistracted by the proposal details. They review the items line by line. During discussions, a marketer should support the process by writing down each assumption, some of which will go in the proposal, and others which may be used during intense negotiations where a firm has to justify its pricing.

If you anticipate that negotiation will go beyond the "big three," for example a protracted discussion of allowable overhead and multipliers, then more preparation will be required. If your math includes special assumptions, then the marketer's role may be to show the math when asked, and to be caretaker of documented backup, such as audited rates, explanations of other direct costs (ODCs), and any other pricing policy.

Many firms have an internal review process, which needs to be factored into the proposal timetable. Also, the documentation of assumptions you worked so hard to prepare should also help you with internal reviews. Proposals with large teams also must obtain accurate pricing and backup information from all subconsultants.

We would also offer a hard-won lesson about price proposals. You may think that there is no other option than to present a single number as your bid, but that may not be true. While it is important to be responsive to the client's RFP, you may be able to provide a price range. However, always accompany it with a discussion that justifies the lower and upper ends of the range. If your client is the type who is willing to consider alternatives, then you might offer scope or price options and alternatives which suit their needs.

Contract terms and conditions

When it comes to contract fine print, your proposal can set you up for easy contract negotiations, or make your life difficult. Some clients include their draft contract with the solicitation, and ask for comments or assurance that your firm is prepared to sign on the bottom line "as-is." This demands that legal and risk review be involved in the proposal process. A risk manager, often an attorney, but also frequently a senior business manager within the firm, may conduct a review of the contract terms, and then develop a pile of comments or requests for changes.

In our experience, any proposal that includes recommended contract changes should be viewed as a sales opportunity, not as legal positioning. The best approach we've seen is to present the proposed changes with an explanation. If at all possible, you should demonstrate all conceivable benefits to the client to make the case that your firm is not selfishly requesting changes. Simply incorporating a "red-lined" version of the client's contract without elaboration is going to go over like a lead balloon.

We caution firms to be extra careful when clients procedurally include your proposal in the contract documents. We recommend against this practice, as proposals are sales documents and not intended to be contractually binding. If you anticipate this will happen, then the marketing team needs to add an additional layer of review. Comb through your submittal from the perspective that it could become the basis of resolving a future dispute. The most common areas of contention are ideas presented in a method of approach which do not find their way to the "official" scope of work, which can result in additional work and potentially a budget overrun.

<u>Additional Negotiations Support Opportunities for Marketers</u>

Though marketers typically are not involved directly in negotiations, the following points may help the marketing team create a better proposal:

- One of our mentors is fond of saying that many technical professionals negotiate with themselves before they negotiate with the client. Another likes to say that "If you don't ask, you won't get." These points are both valid. We find that the art of reaching a proposal price is complicated by technical professionals who lower their price before sitting across the table from the client. Usually this trend is circular, with discussions among the technical team, business developers, and managers driving the price down further and further, until they are doing the project for free just for the prestige of the work. The marketer can facilitate the discussion back to the realm of sanity by asking simple questions such as "What's the client's budget? Has anyone asked?" or "What profit are we expecting from this assignment?" and "at what price would the client be in sticker-shock?"

- In negotiations, each side should be prepared to make concessions in order to receive them in return. That's the definition of a negotiation. Taking a firm stand can result in failed negotiations. We recommend being flexible and working through disagreements by offering alternatives. From the marketer's perspective, this means planning for flexibility. Anticipate the client's hard positions and identify alternatives to be included in the proposal. For example, if your client's contract includes onerous provisions on liability, then your proposal may make a strong case that risky work performed by subconsultants be contracted directly with the client.

- Your firm should never allow the project manager to lead contentious negotiations. The project manager needs to be the client's partner once the project starts. We see most firms getting a negotiator involved, who may be an independent senior manager or contract administrator.

- One of the best concepts we've seen applied to negotiations is called: wish – want – walk[14]. In this approach, "wish" sets a goal for the negotiations, "want" is where the market may dictate the results, and "walk" is where you draw the line and leave the table. We have found this to be a helpful approach to set expectations. By arriving at these parameters, it helps you frame the discussions with the client. Internally, by gaining acceptance early on, expectations will be set that can be helpful in avoiding disappointment. You can refer critics back to the original "wish – want – walk" decisions, as binding conditions.

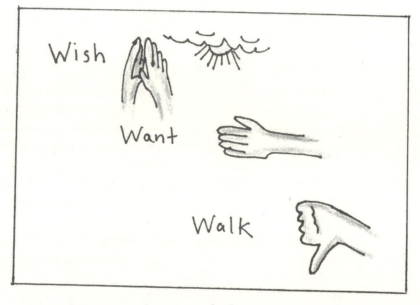

Some clients may take time to finalize contract award. Weeks and months may pass. As marketers, we're always anxious for the signatures to be placed on the bottom line, and for notice to proceed to be received because this finally calls a successful end to the pursuit.

Debrief

Learning from your successes and failures is important for continuous improvement of your marketing processes. A formal debrief offers an opportunity to get inside the client's thought process and understand

---

[14] Donaldson, Michael C. Fearless Negotiating: The Wish-want-walk Method to Reach Solutions That Work. New York: McGraw-Hill, 2007.

their interpretation of your competitive strategies, messages, and other aspects of a pursuit. Some large public agencies provide formal, written debriefs that are extremely useful and need only be requested. Rarely will a client deny your request for a debrief, although some will need a little persuasion. Be persistent, but aware that they have a right to decline.

It is important to designate the right person to conduct a debrief. Your first inclination may be to send in a key member of the project team, such as the project manager. This can be problematic, because many clients' instincts will tend toward politeness, rather than truth (especially if the truth hurts). They may not raise sensitive issues directly to the person to whom it may apply. We typically send senior marketing staff to conduct the debrief. Best case, the marketer was involved in the pursuit, but is not likely to be well-known by the client. The marketer will know the content and strategy of the pursuit, but is less likely to be biased. Certainly, objectivity is important; there is no room for any tone of defensiveness.

> *The concept of "wish – want – walk" is a useful tool for other types of negotiations, as well. For example, a marketer in negotiations for a salary increase or a new position can think in these terms. How much money do you wish you could make? How much would you accept? What's your "floor" position? This should coincide with a process for analyzing what you would be willing to do for that "wish" salary.*

Subject to budgetary considerations, all debriefs should be face-to-face, if possible. They are less effective when performed by telephone, but as a last resort still hold value.

It's important to request a debrief in a timely manner. You might not want to make the request on the day of an unfavorable decision, but we wouldn't let much time pass. Some clients have a policy of not debriefing until the contract negotiations are concluded with the selected firm. Other clients may be willing to talk immediately. Ideally, you should conduct the debrief as soon as possible, while ideas and impressions are fresh in the minds of the client.

Open-ended questions are the best type of inquiry in a debrief. You're attempting to draw out the client beyond a rote response. Ideally, you're testing to see if certain messages came across. If you're not hearing them echoed by the client, this is a concern. Be sure to ask for the client's impressions of how others on the selection committee received the message, and how they reacted, though one person's impressions of another's perspective may be inaccurate. Also, after the open-ended questions, you should test to see how certain ideas were received. Be sure to ask what might have been done differently. Ask how the other firms did; you might not get a response, but it doesn't hurt to ask.

You should be sensitive to the fact that many clients are uncomfortable with debriefs. They often feel as if they are being challenged, something you must not do if you want valuable feedback. Sometimes it is wise to ask for a deliberately short period of time – say 20 minutes – for the debrief. You should also begin by confirming how much time the client has available. Stick to the timetable and look for signs that the meeting may be over early. If the client offers to spend more time, great, but you need to be especially respectful in debrief situations.

Also, be mindful of sensitive information in a loss. Sometimes, decisions can be personal, and can be misinterpreted as hurtful or biased. This knowledge should not be written down, but, rather, handled discretely. Sometimes, the information is accurate, and although damaging, must be used by management to decide if certain staff should be proposed in a similar role for the future. You also need to be mindful of personality conflicts.

We find in some cases that debriefs after a win are even more valuable than for losses. Many times, firms do not perform these, despite the large investment in a proposal and interview. Although the questions are

> Harold played a minor advisory role in an important selection process for the design of a major facility upgrade. The firm was not selected. In fact, a dark horse was ultimately awarded the contract. A formal debrief was conducted, resulting in politically correct responses to questions. Members of our firm's pursuit team walked away puzzled and, needless to say, disappointed.
>
> Almost ten years later, a comment was made in a conversation between a member of our firm and the client's staff. Apparently, the top two contenders had too much work with this client. Politically, it would have been difficult for management to award another contract to either firm despite the fact that they were tied for first place in the scoring.
>
> What a shocker, as we all felt cheated. While it didn't make a difference to the original pursuit team, we were able to win a construction management opportunity for the same facility. At least the team members felt somewhat vindicated in not walking away empty-handed.

similar, you may be surprised at hearing reasons for your selection despite your best competitive strategy and positioning. We also recommend conducting internal discussions on debrief findings. Lessons learned are valuable for everyone involved.

> *I now recollect my experience on the major pursuit for a program management assignment to be an example of a selection committee not fully empowered with the final decision. It was nerve-wracking to sit on the sidelines, hearing bits and pieces of news on how the "big boys" were working the third phase of this pursuit. There were numerous meetings. I later learned that this was an expected, normal part of doing business with this client.*
>
> *It would be several more weeks before the results were announced. Finally, the solution was a shotgun marriage between the top two finishers. Upon reflection, the team of two firms served this client well through an engagement that lasted for many years, so everything worked out nicely.*

Chapter 10
Annotated Bibliography

"It is a good thing for an uneducated man to read good books of quotations."
– Winston Churchill

1. Beckwith, Harry. *Selling the Invisible: A Field Guide to Modern Marketing*. New York: Warner, 1997. Print. One of the first books to address the under-discussed topic of sales within the services industry. There are a surprising number of tricks of the trade which can be applied to the sales of rocket science.

2. "Brand." *Wikipedia*. Wikimedia Foundation, 22 Apr. 2014. Web. 22 Apr. 2014. A solid description of a difficult concept.

3. Cohen, Herb. *You Can Negotiate Anything*. Secaucus, NJ: L. Stuart, 1980. Print. This lays a concrete foundation on building negotiating skills.

4. Collins, James C. *Good to Great: Why Some Companies Make the Leap--and Others Don't*. New York, NY: Harper Business, 2001. Print. Knowing who to "get on the bus" is key to forming any successful team. The makeup of your sales team, both technical and marketers, is crucial to achieving your business development goals. This book shows how the great firms accomplish it.

5. Covey, Sean. *The 7 Habits of Highly Effective Teens: The Miniature Edition: The Ultimate Teenage Success Guide*. Philadelphia: Running, 2002. Print. Helpful for people of any age.

6. Davidow, William H., and Bro Uttal. *Total Customer Service: The Ultimate Weapon*. New York: Harper & Row, 1989. Print. One of the early books to pick up on the power of superior customer service in improving performance and your bottom line.

7. Donaldson, Michael C. *Fearless Negotiating: The Wish-want-walk Method to Reach Solutions That Work*. New York: McGraw-Hill, 2007. Print. The W-W-W method is compelling.

8. Gladwell, Malcolm. *The Tipping Point: How Little Things Can Make a Big Difference.* Boston: Little, Brown, 2000. Print. At first, this book seems more of an explanation of pop culture than applicable to business, but it offers a number of new perspectives on how little things become big. Written before the phrase "going viral" was popularized. We like the explanation of connectors, mavens, and salesmen.

9. Goleman, Daniel, Richard E. Boyatzis, and Annie McKee. *Primal Leadership: Realizing the Power of Emotional Intelligence.* Boston, MA: Harvard Business School, 2002. Print. An important argument in favor of emotions in the business environment. Compares intelligence quotient (IQ) versus the emotional intelligence (EQ) of leaders and their impact on people, organizations, and culture.

10. Green, Charles H. *Trust-based Selling: Using Customer Focus and Collaboration to Build Long-term Relationships.* New York: McGraw-Hill, 2006. Print. By one of the authors of *The Trusted Advisor*, this book takes the concept of selling through trust relationships one step further. As you read this and begin to think about the examples, you'll have that feeling of déjà vu over those extraordinarily successful people you know in the business.

11. Greenleaf, Robert K. *Servant Leadership: A Journey into the Nature of Legitimate Power and Greatness.* New York: Paulist, 1977. Print. Greenleaf's 1970 essay "The Servant as Leader" followed by the book in 1977 were seminal works. One of the best philosophical, almost spiritual, books on how to get people to do the right thing.

12. Heath, Chip, and Dan Heath. *Switch: How to Change Things When Change Is Hard.* New York: Broadway, 2010. Print. We really liked the explanation of how to motivate the feelings (art) of your customers in comparison to their analytical (rocket science) direction. For technology based companies, the authors' tips on managing change when all else fails are spot on.

13. Heskett, James L. *Managing in the Service Economy.* Boston, MA: Harvard Business School, 1986. Print. This is a nice overall look at how to manage a services firm, as opposed to a manufacturing operation. While many business books deal with Fortune 500 or 1000 companies who make products, this book talks about serving something to clients.

14. Hesse, Hermann. *The Journey to the East*. New York: Noonday, 1957. Print. Go ahead, read it, it won't hurt you.

15. Kaplan, Robert S.; Norton, David P., *The Balanced Scorecard*, Harvard Business School Press, 1996. Print. While this doesn't directly apply to business development, sooner or later your management is likely to bring one of these to the table. You should be ready and know what is expected of you in doing your part for the overall company's success.

16. Kim, W. Chan., and Renée Mauborgne. *Blue Ocean Strategy: How to Create Uncontested Market Space and Make the Competition Irrelevant*. Boston, MA: Harvard Business School, 2005. Print. Do you find your technologists looking to copy the competition? Is there a market leader they're trying to imitate? Consider going where the competition isn't and creating a new market where you can be first.

17. Kotter, John P. *Leading Change*. Boston, MA: Harvard Business School, 1996. Print. Over the years, we've probably referred to this book for getting things done more often than any other book. It's a primer on how to change your business to meet new competitive demands in the market place.

18. Maister, David H., Charles H. Green, and Robert M. Galford. *The Trusted Advisor*. New York: Free, 2000. Print. We are often asked if there were only one relevant book to read, what would we recommend? This book is it. More than any other book, The Trusted Advisor bridges the gap between simply solving your client's problems to becoming one of their inner circle of advisors. If you can truly understand the nature of superior professional relationships, then you'll be ahead of the pack in balancing art with rocket science.

19. Maister, David. *Managing the Professional Service Firm*. London: Free Business, 2003. Print. By one of the authors of The Trusted Advisor. It is one of the few books which take an analytical look at successful models for organizing and running a consulting firm. Most business books focus on large manufacturing or non-professional service companies.

20. Merrill, David W., and Roger H. Reid. *Personal Styles & Effective Performance*. Radnor, PA: Chilton Book, 1981. Print. These authors delve into basic personality types and the characteristics of behav-

ior. More importantly, they lay the foundation for approaching the art of persuading each personality type, as they are decidedly different from one another.

21. Miller, Arthur. *Death of a Salesman*. New York: Penguin, 1996. Print. Goes without saying, a classic.

22. Naisbitt, John. *Megatrends: Ten New Directions Transforming Our Lives*. New York: Warner, 1982. Print. This is an oldie but goodie and offers insights to the future. It is surprising how many of these predictions came true (and how many did not). Nonetheless, it is a worthwhile exercise in thinking ahead of your market place and planning accordingly.

23. Potter, Robert A. *Winning in the Invisible Market: A Guide to Selling Professional Services in the Turbulent times*. United States: R.A. Potter, 2003. Print. One of the first authors to recognize the abstract nature of services, and how sales must be approached differently than for consumer goods and non-technical services.

24. Rose, Stuart W. *Mandeville: A Guide for the Marketing of Professional Services*. Washington, D.C.: Professional Development Resources, 1995. Print. Expert book on the art of listening.

25. Sun Tzu, and Samuel B. Griffith. *The Art of War*. London: Oxford UP, 1971. Print. Popularized in the movie Wall Street, this book has been reprinted many times. It's a short, but worthwhile read of some ancient concepts which still apply to competing in today's markets.

26. Surowiecki, James. *The Wisdom of Crowds: Why the Many Are Smarter than the Few and How Collective Wisdom Shapes Business, Economies, Societies, and Nations*. New York: Doubleday, 2004. Print. If you're either looking to sell to a large market or trying to understand an internal issue, read this book. It does a nice job of explaining how two (or many more) heads are better than one.

27. Weitz, Barton A. "Effectiveness in Sales Interactions: A Contingency Framework." *Journal of Marketing* 45.1 (1981): 85. Print.

28. Weitz, Barton A., Harish Sujan, and Mita Sujan. "Knowledge, Motivation, and Adaptive Behavior: A Framework for Improving Selling Effectiveness." Journal of Marketing 50.4 (1986): 174. Print.

ABOUT THE AUTHORS

Charles McIntyre is Director of Marketing for an electrical and technology construction firm. He has worked in the technical professional services industry for more than 20 years, and is a member of the Society of Marketing Professional Services (SMPS). As a non-technical professional in a highly technical world, he bridges the gap between the art of persuasion and the science of technical solutions.

Harold Glaser is Director of Client Excellence with an engineering and environmental science firm. As a consultant, he has worked with some of the largest utilities and agencies in the world. With over 30 years of experience as a civil engineer, the emphasis of his career has been on business development. He is a Registered Professional Engineer, Life Member of the American Water Works Association, and a Member of the American Society of Civil Engineers.

Made in the USA
Las Vegas, NV
04 June 2021